LEVEL C

Comprehension PLUS

Dr. Diane Lapp
Dr. James Flood

Modern Curriculum Press

13,14,15,58,59,97: Michael Reid. 18,19,37,38,40,50,52,89,90,91: Liz Allen. 21,22,23,101,102: Julie Durrell.
25: Rosiland Solomon. 29,30,31,32: Ellen Joy Sasaki. 105,106: Stacy Peterson. 61,62: Patrick Girouard.
70,77,78,123: Deirdre Newman. 81,82,83: Liisa Chauncy Guida. 85,86,88,118,120: Judy Love.

5: Charles D. Winters/Photo Researchers. 6(t): B.&C Alexander/Photo Researchers.
6(b): American Stock/Archive Photos. 7: SuperStock.
9: Wayne Eastep/Tony Stone Images. 10(t.l): Mark C. Burnett/ Photo Researchers.
10(t.r): Ross M. Horowitz/Image Bank. 10(b): PhotoDisc.
17: Caggiano/Stockfood America. 26: Alan R. Moller/Tony Stone Images.
33: Carolyn A. McKeone/ Photo Researchers. 34, 98(r): Tim Flach/Tony Stone Images.
36: Phil A. Dotson/ Photo Researchers. 41: David Young Wolf/Tony Stone Images.
42: Scott Cunningham/NBA/Allsport. 45: Doug Armand/Tony Stone Images.
49: Bettman/Corbis. 53: Stephen Krasemann/ Photo Researchers.
54(t): David Barrow/Earth Scenes. 54(b): Tom Tietz/Tony Stone Images.
56: Robert Winslow/Animals Animals. 57: Lori Adamski Peek/Tony Stone Images.
65(t): Steven M. Barnett/Liaison International. 66: Jack Fields/Corbis.
69: Phil Lauro/Index Stock Imagery. 70(b): Phil Degginger/Earth Scenes.
71: Peggy/Yoram Kahana/Peter Arnold. 73: James Balog/Tony Stone Images.
74: Michael Dick/Animals Animals. 75: Tom Brakefield/Corbis.
93: Keith Kent/ Photo Researchers. 94(t): Richard Nowitz/ Photo Researchers.
94(b): Keith Foster/ Photo Researchers. 98(l): Thomas D.W. Friedman/ Photo Researchers.
107: Ron Austing/ Photo Researchers. 109: K.Iwasaki/The Stock Market.
110: NASA/The Stock Market. 112: DRA/Still Pictures/Peter Arnold.
116: Jose Carillo/PhotoEdit. 117: Kennan Ward/The Stock Market.
121: Uniphoto Picture Agency. 122: Ed Reschke/Peter Arnold.

Cover art: photo montage: Wendy Wax. background: Doug Bowles.

Design development: MKR Design, New York: Manuela Paul, Deirdre Newman, Marta K. Ruliffson.

ISBN: 0-7652-2182-9
Printed in the United States of America

11 12 13 14 15   09 08 07 06 05

Table of Contents

Comprehending Text

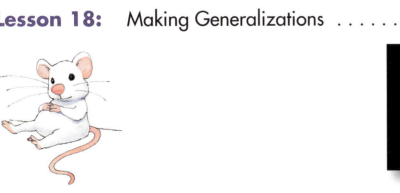

Story Structure

Word Study

Document Reading

Drawing Conclusions

As you read a story or an article, look for details to figure out things an author wants you to know but does not tell you. If you make your own decisions about ideas the author does not tell, then you are **drawing conclusions**.

You may draw conclusions about how characters feel or act or why an event took place. Your conclusions should be based on what you read, what you know, and what makes sense. Being able to draw conclusions will help you understand why certain things happen in a story or an article.

Read the story below. Draw conclusions about the ball game.

In the bottom of the ninth inning, the Hornets were leading 7 to 4. The Jays had two outs. With three Jays on base and Lefty "Homer" Brooks at bat, anything could happen. Deep in right field, Shawna punched her glove.

CRACK! Shawna squinted into the bright sky until the spinning circle appeared, as tiny as a golf ball. She held her breath as it got closer and closer.

Shawna leaped and reached. Suddenly she felt the sting of a catch. Grinning, she ran to join her teammates.

Use story details to draw conclusions about the character, Shawna. Write your answers on the lines.

What team is Shawna on?

_____

What did she do to help her team?

_____

How does Shawna feel at the end? How can you tell?

_____

_____

> ## Tip
>
> Always be ready to back up your conclusion with information from the story or article and other reasons you know.

PLAY BALL!

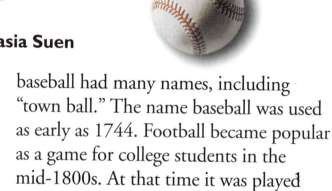

by Anastasia Suen

People have been playing ball games in North America for centuries. Some of the games are very old, while some are more modern.

Hundreds of years ago, people of many different Native American nations played a game with a ball and a stick. The ball was made from animal skin. The top of the stick had a loop. Inside the loop was a net made from leather strips. The game was played on a large field with a goal at each end. Hundreds of people played at once, tossing the ball in the air from stick to stick.

The ball and stick game had many different names. French settlers called it "la crosse" because the stick looked like a cross. Today we call the game lacrosse.

People who came from other countries to live in America brought their own ball games with them. Both baseball and football grew out of games that had been played in England. Early American baseball had many names, including "town ball." The name baseball was used as early as 1744. Football became popular as a game for college students in the mid-1800s. At that time it was played more like soccer is played today.

In 1891, a college gym teacher in Massachusetts wanted to create a sport that his students could play indoors during the winter. He remembered a rock-throwing game he played as a child called "Duck on a Rock." He made up new rules and hung two peach baskets on the wall of the gym. That is how basketball was invented.

Today we play many ball games—some old, some new, and all of them fun.

Checking Comprehension

Write the answer to each question on the lines.

1. What is the most important idea you want to remember from reading this article?

   _____

   _____

2. How are ball games from around the world alike and different?

   _____

   _____

Practicing Comprehension Skills

Fill in the circle to complete the sentence or answer the question.

3. In the Native American ball-and-stick game, the players probably _____ .

   ○ played on teams   ○ hit the ball over a net

   ○ played on horseback   ○ called their game lacrosse

4. What detail helped you figure this out?

   ○ Some games are very old.   ○ The ball was made from animal skin.

   ○ Two goals were used.   ○ The ball was tossed in the air.

5. The game of basketball probably got its name from _____ .

   ○ Native American baskets   ○ fruit baskets

   ○ a basket maker   ○ a ball that looked like a basket

6. What detail helped you figure this out?

   ○ Students played indoors.   ○ The game was played in a gym.

   ○ It's like "Duck on a Rock."   ○ Peach baskets were used.

Look at the diagram. Think about the details from the article. Add something you know about the history of baseball. Then write a conclusion.

Details	What I Know	Conclusion
Baseball grew out of games from England.	When something grows, it usually changes.	_____
Baseball was called "Town Ball" in early America.	_____ _____	_____ _____ _____ _____ _____

Practicing Vocabulary

Write the word from the box that matches each clue.

| animal   baskets   centuries   invented   leather   modern   nations |

_____   **7.**   dog, bird, or snake

_____   **8.**   containers

_____   **9.**   made for the first time

_____   **10.**   material made from skins

_____   **11.**   Canada, England, and India

_____   **12.**   hundreds of years

_____   **13.**   opposite of *old*

Writing Sentences About a Sport
On another piece of paper, write sentences that tell about a sport. Give clues about the sport, but don't tell what sport it is. Then let a friend read your sentences and draw a conclusion to decide what sport you wrote about.

Sequence: Order of Events

The events that happen in a story follow a **sequence**, or order. When you read, it is important to keep track of the sequence of events so that you can better understand the story. One way to follow the sequence of events in a story is to look for words such as *first, next, then,* and *finally*. Dates and times of day can also be clues to help you see the sequence, for example *in the morning* or *on Saturday*. When there are no clue words, you can picture the story events in your mind and ask yourself what happens *first, next,* and *last*.

Read the story. Think about the order in which things happen.

"I've got a serious problem," Jacob complained to his friend Pam one afternoon. "I'm excited about our talent show but can't think of anything to do."

Pam thought for a moment, "I wanted to be in the show, too. At first I didn't know what to do either. Then I remembered that I like to sing. Wouldn't it be fun to sing a song in the talent show? I selected my favorite song, and I practiced by singing it everyday."

Jacob quickly interrupted, "But, Pam, I can't sing!"

"Then what can you do? Think of something you enjoy."

"I've got an idea!" Jacob replied with a grin. "I'll tell jokes in the talent show. All our friends will enjoy a good laugh!"

Write a number from 1 to 5 to show the story events in order.

_____ Jacob came up with an idea.

_____ Pam told Jacob how she got ready for the show.

_____ Jacob told Pam he had a problem.

_____ Pam explained how she chose her talent.

_____ Pam told Jacob to think of something he enjoys.

Tip

When you read, ask yourself, *Would the story have ended differently if the events had happened in a different order?*

Sparky THE WONDER DOG

I was convinced that my dog Sparky would be good at performing tricks in the school talent show. I had one week to train him.

First I placed a single dog biscuit under a can and put out two other cans with no biscuits under them. Then I mixed up the cans, so Sparky wouldn't know which one had the biscuit under it. Curiously, he sniffed each can. Then he flipped over the middle can and found the biscuit! "Excellent job!" I praised.

Next I had to teach Sparky how to jump through a hoop. I held the hoop in front of him and commanded, "Jump, Sparky!" He just sat there. He had no idea what he was supposed to do. Then I remembered that Sparky knew how to fetch a ball. Tossing a ball through the hoop, I said, "Jump, Sparky!" Sparky followed the ball and jumped through the hoop. Quickly, I rewarded him with a dog biscuit.

We practiced this way all week. At the end of the week I hid the ball, held up the hoop, and said, "Jump, Sparky!" Believe it or not, Sparky jumped right through the hoop. I was so proud that I gave him two biscuits and a big hug. We had done it. I was confident Sparky the Wonder Dog was going to be a huge hit with the audience at the show!

Checking Comprehension

1. If you could ask Pat what she learned from training Sparky, what do you think she would tell you?

   _____

   _____

2. Will Sparky be a hit at the show? Explain your answer.

   _____

   _____

Practicing Comprehension Skills

Write a number from 1 to 8 to show the sequence of events in "Sparky the Wonder Dog."

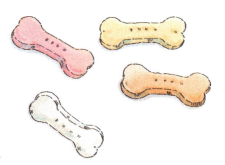

3. ____ Sparky jumps through the hoop on his own.

4. ____ First Pat teaches Sparky a hide-the-biscuit trick.

5. ____ Pat decides to teach Sparky tricks for a show.

6. ____ On the day of the show, Pat and Sparky feel ready.

7. ____ Next Pat wants Sparky to jump through a hoop.

8. ____ Pat tosses a ball through the hoop for Sparky to follow.

9. ____ At the end of the week, Pat hides the ball.

10. ____ Pat and Sparky practice the hoop trick all week.

11. What word clues help you know the sequence?

   _____

   _____

12. What do you think might have happened if Pat had not thrown the ball through the hoop?

_____

13. What might have been different if the show was a week earlier?

_____

14. What might be different if Pat had not rewarded Sparky with biscuits?

_____

Practicing Vocabulary

Choose the word from the box that best replaces the underlined word or words. Write the word on the line.

audience	biscuit	confident	flipped	followed	tossing	train

_____ **15.** Pat was <u>sure</u> Sparky could get a ball.

_____ **16.** Pat was <u>throwing</u> a ball through a hoop.

_____ **17.** A smart dog is easy to <u>teach</u>.

_____ **18.** Sparky <u>chased</u> the ball.

_____ **19.** Sparky's reward was a <u>treat</u>.

_____ **20.** Sparky <u>turned</u> over the can with the biscuit underneath.

_____ **21.** The <u>people watching</u> loved Sparky's tricks.

Writing a Narrative Paragraph
Imagine you will perform in a talent show. Write a paragraph that tells what you will do to get ready for the show. You may want to use words like _first, next,_ and _last_ to help your readers see the sequence of events.

Sequence: Steps in a Process

When you read an article or story, what happens first? What happens next? What happens last? These are important questions to keep in mind when you are reading about how to do something.

When you read about how to do something, look for clue words like *first*, *next*, *then*, and *finally*. They are clues that will help you understand the order in which things happen.

Read the following article. As you read, keep in mind what you should do first, next, and so on.

Did you know you can make pizza at home? Before you begin, ask a grown-up for help. Then gather the ingredients. You will need a piece of pita bread, one-half cup of spaghetti sauce, a few chopped vegetables, such as green pepper, mushrooms, or tomatoes, and one-half cup of grated mozzarella cheese.

The first step is to heat the oven to 350°. Then, spread the sauce on the bread. Next, sprinkle on the vegetables and top the pizza with cheese. Before you put your pizza in the oven, put a little more sauce on top. Finally, bake it for six to eight minutes. The last step is to EAT IT UP!

Below are the steps for making pizza at home. They are not in order. Write a number from 1-5 to show the right order.

____ Put the pizza in the oven and bake for six to eight minutes.

____ Sprinkle on vegetables and top with cheese.

____ Heat the oven.

____ Ask a grown-up for help.

____ Spread sauce on the bread.

Tip

Look for clue words like *first*, *next*, *then*, *before*, *after*, and *finally* when you are trying to figure out the sequence of events in a story.

Read the story about a famous pizza chef. Think about the steps Chef Pigaletto uses to make pizza.

The Big Pig PIZZA

by Trinka Hakes Noble

Chef Pigaletto wanted to be the most famous pizza chef in the world. He decided to make a pizza like no other. "I'll call it the Big Pig Pizza!" he said.

First Chef Pigaletto made a giant crust as big as a trampoline. He imagined his picture on the front page of the *Hog World News*. Next, he poured on gallons of sauce and heaped on mounds of cheese while he practiced smiling. He wanted to be ready when the photographers took his picture.

Then, Chef Pigaletto used pounds of meatballs to spell out his name in big letters: PIGALETTO. He wanted to make sure the newspaper headlines printed his name the right way.

Finally the pizza was ready to be baked, but Chef Pigaletto had a problem. The huge pizza didn't fit inside the oven. He stayed up all night making his oven bigger and planning what he'd wear for his photographs.

The next morning he finally put the Big Pig Pizza into the oven. By noon his masterpiece was ready for the world to see. There was just one problem. Chef Pigaletto had been so busy making the pizza that he had forgotten to eat.

Suddenly, he was so hungry that he ate up the whole pizza.

The Big Pig Pizza never made Chef Pigaletto world famous. It did make him the world's biggest pig!

Checking Comprehension

Write the answer to each question on the lines.

1. What did Chef Pigaletto do to try to become famous?

   _____

   _____

2. Why didn't Chef Pigaletto's plan work?

   _____

   _____

Practicing Comprehension Skills

3. Read each sentence. On the line before each sentence, write a number from 1 to 7 to show the sequence of events in "The Big Pig Pizza."

   ____ Chef Pigaletto's pizza didn't fit in the oven.

   ____ Chef Pigaletto decided to make the Big Pig Pizza.

   ____ First he made the crust.

   ____ Chef Pigaletto became the world's biggest pig.

   ____ Suddenly, Chef Pigaletto was very hungry.

   ____ Then he added sauce, cheese, and meatballs.

   ____ Chef Pigaletto wanted to become famous.

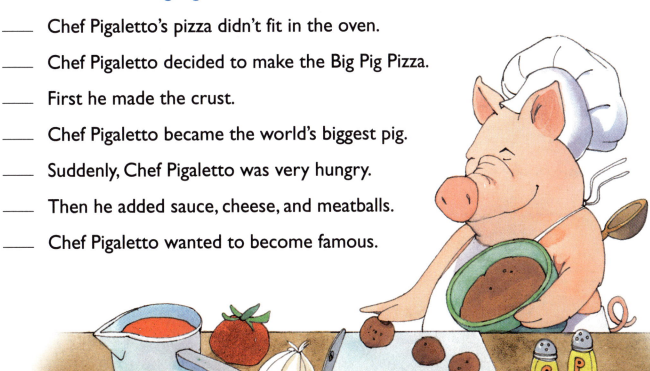

STRATEGY: Sequence: Steps in a Process

Fill in the circle before the right answer.

4. What did Chef Pigaletto do first?

○ He made a
giant crust.

○ He put the pizza
into the oven.

○ He spelled out his
name in meatballs.

5. What did Chef Pigaletto do after he put
meatball letters on the Big Pig Pizza?

○ He poured on
gallons of sauce.

○ He heaped
on cheese.

○ He found out the
oven was too small.

Practicing Vocabulary

Write a word from the box to finish each sentence.

crust	famous	newspaper	chef	giant	imagined	masterpiece

6. Everyone knew who the woman was because she was so _____ .

7. The artist was proud of his painting and called it a _____ .

8. The _____ was making one of her tastiest dishes.

9. The small plate wasn't big enough for the _____ cake.

10. The little boy _____ that he was driving a fire engine.

11. The woman wrote an article for the _____ .

12. The _____ of the bread is my favorite part.

Writing a How-To Paragraph
On another piece of paper, write a short how-to paragraph
that tells how to make your favorite healthy snack.
Remember to use clue words to tell the order of the steps.

Predicting Outcomes

When you read a story or an article, think about what might happen next. There are often clues that will help you decide what is going to happen next. When you use these clues you are making predictions. This means that you are predicting before you read and while you are reading. Your prediction is what you said would happen. The best way to make **predictions** is to use information you already know and to pay attention to word clues and picture clues.

Before you read, predict what the story might be about. As you read, predict what you think might happen next.

Desert Morning

One morning Sally and her dad were walking in the desert. They observed many rocks and plants, but they hadn't seen any animals. Dad explained that the animals were hiding under rocks, under plants, and in the sand, trying to stay cool.

Suddenly Sally spotted a silver and brown snake perched on a rock. Dad said, "That snake is called a shovelnose because it digs down fast in the sand." The pair kept walking. When Sally turned around, the snake had disappeared. She searched in every direction, but it seemed to have disappeared into thin air.

What did you predict this story would be about? Why?

_____

_____

If Sally and her dad take another walk in the evening, what might they see?

_____

What clues helped you make this prediction?

_____

Tip

After you make a prediction, read on to see if you are correct. If not, go back to find clues that you may have missed.

On Your Own Read the title and look at the picture. Fill in the Before Reading section of the chart on page 23 to make a prediction. As you read, use word clues to check your prediction.

WHERE IS IGGY?

Sara was upset. It was her week to feed the class pets, and Iggy the Iguana was missing. When she had fed the animals yesterday, Iggy had been in his tank. But now he was gone. Her teacher, Ms. Choi, and the other students had looked under desks, on shelves, and in drawers. Iggy was nowhere to be found.

Ms. Choi asked Sara to review what she had done with the animals the day before. Sara explained that she had fed the rabbit, the fish, and the turtles first. Next she had fed Iggy. She had given him an iguana salad of vegetables, fruit, and grain, and had then tossed in a few rose petals, since Iggy loved roses.

Ms. Choi asked Sara if she had latched the screen on top of Iggy's tank. Sara turned pale and gulped. She couldn't remember. Because iguanas can fit into very small spaces, she knew Iggy had probably squeezed out. He could be anywhere by now!

Suddenly the classroom door flew open. Mrs. Carter, the science teacher, burst in and said, "Thank you for taking care of my rose bushes while I was gone last week. They look beautiful."

Ms. Choi snapped her fingers. She knew exactly where Iggy was! Sara and the other students followed her as she marched into the science lab next door. Rose plants filled the room. Ms. Choi moved some flowerpots away from the wall. There was Iggy, happily chewing on a rose petal. He wasn't lost; he was just enjoying a little extra dessert.

Checking Comprehension

Write the answer to each question on the lines.

1. What problem does Ms. Choi's class have?
    How is it solved?

    _____

2. Why does Sara think it's her fault that Iggy is missing?

    _____

Practicing Comprehension Skills

3. Look at the chart. Read the prediction you made before reading
    the story. Now finish the chart. Write what you know happened.
    Does your prediction match what happened?

Before Reading	After Reading
What I Predict Will Happen _____ _____ _____	**What I Know Happened** _____ _____ _____
Why I Think That Will Happen _____ _____ _____	**What Might Happen Next** _____ _____ _____

4. Which two story clues helped you predict that Iggy was in the science lab?

○ Rose bushes are in the lab.　　○ Students checked the classroom.

○ Iggy loves to eat roses.　　○ Iggy eats vegetables and grains.

5. Which story clues help you predict what might happen next?

○ Ms. Choi asked Sara if she had latched the screen.　　○ Iguanas can squeeze through very small places.

○ Ms. Choi knew where Iggy was.　　○ Mrs. Carter thanked the students for taking care of her roses.

Practicing Vocabulary

Choose a word from the box that best matches each definition.
Write the word on the line.

grain	gulped	iguana	latched	pale	petals	tank

_____ **6.** a lizard with a ridge down its back

_____ **7.** faint in color, whitish

_____ **8.** glass box for keeping an animal

_____ **9.** closed or fastened securely

_____ **10.** colored parts of a flower

_____ **11.** kernel of corn or wheat

_____ **12.** swallowed loudly

Writing a Story
Imagine that your class has lost a pet. Write a short story to tell what happens. Read the first part of your story to a partner. Ask him or her to predict how it will end. Then finish reading.

Recognizing Cause and Effect

When you read a story or an article, do you stop to think about what happens and why things happen? A **cause** is a reason why something happens. An **effect** is what happens. Recognizing causes and effects will help you understand how the events in a story or details in an article fit together.

Clue words such as *so, because,* and *since* help point out causes and effects. When there are no clue words, ask yourself the questions: *What happened?* and *Why did this happen?* Sometimes there can be more than one cause or effect.

Read the following experiment. Think about what happens and why it happens.

You can make a model of a tornado in a jar. In this experiment, the "rain" is water mixed with vinegar and liquid soap. The motion you make is like the movement of air in a tornado.

Fill a large jar three quarters full of water. Add 2 drops of food coloring, 1 teaspoon of liquid soap, and 1 teaspoon of vinegar. Tighten the lid. Shake the jar hard. Then give the jar a good twist. The liquid will form a cone that looks like a small tornado.

Think about what happens in this experiment and why it happens. Write the answers on the lines.

What happens when you shake and twist the jar?

_____

_____

What causes this to happen?

_____

_____

Tip

Recognizing causes and effects can help you understand and remember what you read.

A Powerful Spinning Wind

Tornadoes are very powerful spinning winds that can form below clouds during strong thunderstorms. Tornadoes begin when warm, moist air gets trapped between a layer of cold, dry air above and a layer of warm, dry air below. The warm air gets pulled up into the thundercloud. Air pressure in the storm is very low, which causes the air to spin. It spins faster and faster and takes the shape of a funnel or cone. We can see tornadoes, or twisters, because dust is sucked up with the air.

Tornadoes are very dangerous, since they move so fast. The spinning winds inside a tornado can reach 500 miles per hour. The strong spinning wind is like a vacuum cleaner. Objects under this swirling funnel get pulled up inside it. A tornado can pick up huge objects like trees, trucks, and houses. When these objects land, they can smash and crush things. Buildings can explode inside a tornado because the air pressure in the tornado is so low and the air pressure inside the buildings is higher. This causes the air inside the buildings to burst out in an explosion.

Tornadoes usually happen during the spring and summer. They can strike at any time of day, but they are more common in the late afternoon and evening, after the heat of the day has built up.

Checking Comprehension

Write the answer to each question on the lines.

1. What makes a tornado different from a very strong wind?

   _____

   _____

2. Why are tornadoes so dangerous?

   _____

   _____

Practicing Comprehension Skills

Reread the article on tornadoes. Choose effects from the box to fill in the diagram. Then use the diagram to explain what happens during a tornado.

The air forms a funnel.	Buildings explode.	Air begins to spin.

Cause		
Air pressure is very low.	The air spins faster and faster.	Air pressure is lower inside the tornado and higher in buildings that get pulled in.

Effect		
3. _____ _____	4. _____	5. _____ _____

6. What are *two* things that cause a tornado to form? Fill in the circles.

○ Warm, wet air gets trapped between layers of cold and warm dry air.

○ Rain mixes with clouds and dust.

○ It rains very hard, and there is thunder.

○ Warm air gets pulled up, and it spins around.

Write the cause in your own words.

7. Tornadoes are dangerous because _____

_____

Practicing Vocabulary

Write a word from the box to finish each sentence.

funnel	moist	pressure	spinning	thunderstorm	tornado	explosion

8. Mary thought the damp air felt very hot and _____ .

9. The weather forecast was for a strong _____ .

10. Then Mary saw something shaped like a cone or _____ .

11. The funnel shape was _____ around very fast.

12. Mary feared the air _____ was building in her house.

13. She opened some windows to avoid an _____ .

14. Mary knew a _____ had formed in the strong storm.

Writing a News Report
Pretend you are a news reporter. It has just snowed for twelve hours. Three feet of snow are on the ground. What would the effects be? On another piece of paper, write a news report.

Fantasy and Realistic Stories

Did you know that all stories come from a writer's imagination and that not all stories are the same? Some stories are about characters who are like people you know. These characters talk and act like real people. We call this a **realistic story** because it tells about something that could happen. Other stories are make-believe. A **fantasy** is a story about something that could not happen in real life. In a fantasy, animals might talk and think like people, unreal things might happen, or the story could tell about things that really wouldn't happen in the future.

Read the two stories below. Decide which one is a realistic story and which one is a fantasy.

Story 1

While walking in the woods one day, Emily saw a shiny red ring on the ground. "Wow, that's beautiful," she thought. While examining the ring, she noticed the initials ZH inside. "This must belong to the new girl, Zena Hall," she thought. "I'll call her right away."

Story 2

One afternoon, Maddie Mouse went strolling through the forest. Looking down, she noticed a red ring sparkling on the ground. "This must be Raccoon's," she said aloud, "because Raccoon adores shiny things." Maddie headed straight for Raccoon's house to give her the ring.

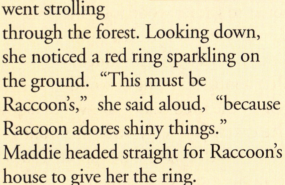

Circle the answer to tell what kind of story each one is.

Story 1
realistic story   fantasy

Story 2
realistic story   fantasy

Tip

To decide if a story is realistic or a fantasy, ask yourself if the things that happen in the story could happen in real life.

The Old Man and the Rice

One chilly morning, a man went into the forest to gather wood for a fire. His thoughtful wife had packed some delicious rice cakes for his lunch.

After a long morning of wood chopping, the tired man sat down to enjoy the rice cakes. Suddenly, two cakes rolled out of his lunch box and disappeared into a hole in the ground. The man raced to get them, but he stopped suddenly when he heard music coming from the hole.

Rolling, rolling, rice cakes,
Very, very nice cakes!

"What a beautiful song," thought the man as he peered into the hole, leaning over so far that he lost his balance and fell to the bottom. After landing, the man looked up and saw hundreds of little mice.

"Thank you for the delicious rice cakes," said one mouse gratefully. "Now please accept this," it said as it handed the man a small bag of rice.

While the mice rolled the man out of the hole, they sang:

Rolling, rolling rice man,
Very, very nice man!

When the proud man finally reached the top, he raced home. "That's a lovely little bag of rice," his wife noticed, "but it's too small to do us much good." However, after she poured the rice into a bowl, the bag was still full. To everyone's surprise, it continued in this way again, and again, and again. Soon, the man and his wife had enough rice to last the rest of their lives, all because of some thankful little mice.

Checking Comprehension

Write the answer to each question on the lines.

1. Why did the mice give the man a gift?

   _____

   _____

2. If the man had not shared his rice cakes with the mice,
   how might the story ending be different?

   _____

   _____

Practicing Comprehension Skills

Read each story event. Put a ✔ by events that could not really happen.

_____ 3. A man chops wood for a fire.

_____ 4. A man peers into a hole.

_____ 5. Hundreds of mice say thank you.

_____ 6. The mice roll the man out of the hole.

_____ 7. The man brings home a bag of rice.

_____ 8. The small bag of rice lasts forever.

_____ 9. Mice were singing a beautiful song.

_____ 10. The wife pours the rice into a bowl.

_____ 11. The mice give a gift to the man.

_____ 12. A man sees many mice.

_____ 13. Rice cakes fall out of a lunch box.

STRATEGY: Distinguishing Fantasy and Realism

14. Is the story about the rolling rice cakes a realistic story or a fantasy?

_____

15. How do you know?

_____

_____

_____

_____

Practicing Vocabulary

Choose a word from the box that best matches each clue.
Write the word on the line.

suddenly	accept	continued	delicious	proud	gratefully	noticed

_____ **16.** tasty

_____ **17.** saw or watched

_____ **18.** happy with oneself

_____ **19.** quickly

_____ **20.** with thanks

_____ **21.** went on

_____ **22.** take

Writing a Fantasy
Write a story that tells about something that isn't real on another piece of paper. Remember that this kind of story is a fantasy. Include details that could not happen in real life. You might include unreal events or animals that talk.

Using Context Clues

What do you do when you are reading and come to a word you do not know? You can read other words or sentences around the unknown word to find clues that will help you figure out the meaning of the word. These words or sentences are called context clues.

Use context clues to help you figure out the meaning of the word *outback*.

Many interesting baby animals live in the wild, bushy outback of Australia.

The words *baby animals live* tell you that the outback is a home for animals. The words *wild* and *bushy* tell you that the outback is not a city but is an open area with many plants.

As you read about a special lizard, use context clues to figure out the meaning of new words.

Do you know the name for this unusual lizard? This is a baby bearded dragon. It lives in the deserts and woods of central Australia. It started life as an egg. Early in June, its mother dug a shallow nest in the sand and laid 16 eggs. Three months later, the babies hatched. The mother was not there because the babies were ready to be on their own and live independently right away. A baby bearded dragon does not really have a beard. Its throat puffs out to scare away animal predators that might want to eat it.

Use the context clues to help decide what each word means. Circle the correct meaning.

I think *independently* means ———— .

a. in the desert   **b.** without any help
c. with their mother   **d.** friendly

I think *predators* means ———— .

a. other bearded dragons   **b.** beards

c. animals that eat other animals   **d.** eggs

Tip

When you come to a word you do not know, read to the end of the sentence for context clues. Also read the sentences before and after the new word to help you figure out the meaning.

Read about another baby animal that lives in Australia. Use context clues to figure out the meaning of words you do not know.

A Baby Named Joey

Most babies are small, but a baby kangaroo, or joey, is as tiny as a grape when it is born. A joey is a special baby, and it grows in a special way.

Kangaroos are Australian mammals known as marsupials. This means that they are animals who carry their young in a pouch on the mother's belly. When a little joey is born, it cannot see or hear, and it has no bones and no fur. It is too helpless to leave its mother. Before the joey is born, the mother licks a trail across her belly, cleaning it thoroughly. The joey crawls along this trail to a fold of skin like a pocket. Inside this pouch, the joey begins to drink milk from its mother. It feels protected and very secure in the safety of this warm, dark place.

In time the joey grows fur and can see and hear. When the joey is about six months old, it sticks its head out of the pouch. When the mother bends down to eat some grass, the joey eats some, too.

Soon the joey begins to leave the pouch for a short time each day. At first it is very shy. When a joey is frightened, it sometimes dives back into its mother's pouch, then peeks out to see if it is safe. Joeys are not afraid of each other! They are very playful and love to have fun and frolic. Sometimes they even box with each other!

When the joey grows up, it may be 5 to 10 feet tall and weigh as much as 200 pounds. Its back legs and feet and its long tail become very strong. With a push from its legs and a boost from its tail, an adult kangaroo usually covers from 5 to 10 feet with each leap. The joey that once was as tiny as a grape has grown into an amazing adult kangaroo.

Checking Comprehension

1. Why does the joey need to live in its mother's pouch?

_____

_____

2. What new things do you think the joey will learn to do when it gets old enough to leave its mother's pouch?

_____

_____

Practicing Comprehension Skills

Use context clues to figure out the meaning of each word.
Fill in the circle next to the meaning.

3. *Marsupials* means ——— .

- ○ female animals that are mammals
- ○ animals who carry babies in a pouch
- ○ helpless animals
- ○ very small animals

4. *Joey* means ——— .

- ○ a baby kangaroo
- ○ a trail
- ○ protected and secure
- ○ a pouch

5. *Secure* means ——— .

- ○ furry
- ○ safe
- ○ black
- ○ cold

6. *Pouch* means ——— .

- ○ punch
- ○ sofa
- ○ blanket
- ○ pocket

7. *Frolic* means ——— .

- ○ run and play
- ○ be afraid
- ○ eat
- ○ fight

What story words helped you know the meanings of these words?
Circle the context clues you used. You may circle more than one
context clue for each word.

8. marsupials

   animals   cannot see   helpless   carry their young in a pouch

9. secure

   safety   protected   dark place   milk

10. pouch

   trail   pocket   fold of skin   warm, dark place

11. frolic

   playful   not afraid   have fun   safe

☀ Practicing Vocabulary

Write a word from the box to finish the sentences in the paragraph.

A _____ is born to a mother kangaroo.
The _____ joey is _____, so it follows
a _____ to its mother's pouch. As the joey grows, it
becomes more _____ and sometimes leaves the pouch.
If a strange animal comes along, the _____ joey quickly
_____ back into its mother's pouch to be safe.

> dives
> helpless
> joey
> trail
> playful
> shy
> tiny

Writing a Letter
On another piece of paper, write a letter to a friend.
Tell your friend about a baby animal you have seen.
Use plenty of clues to explain new words.

Comparing and Contrasting

When you read, do you ever think about how things in the story are the same or different? When you look at two things to see how they are alike or different, you are **comparing** and **contrasting** them. As you read, clue words can signal things that are being compared and contrasted. Words that show how things are alike are *same, both, like,* and *as.* Some words that show contrast are *different, however,* and *but.*

Comparing and contrasting can help you understand characters or events in a story. Writers may compare and contrast for you, or you may do this yourself.

Read the story about Cherie. Think about how the writer compares and contrasts two places.

Cherie was stumped. Her best friend, Maria, had invited her to spend a week at Lake Longhorn, but it was the same week as Space Camp®! Cherie had always dreamed of becoming an astronaut someday.

At Lake Longhorn, Cherie would be able to fish, swim, and sleep outdoors. On the other hand, at Space Camp, she might get to spend time in a real space capsule. Both trips would be a lot of fun, but at Space Camp she would learn a lot, too. What should she do?

Write one way Space Camp and Lake Longhorn are the same.

_____

Write one way Space Camp and Lake Longhorn are different.

_____

_____

_____

> ## Tip
>
> Remember to compare and contrast things as you read. Think about how the characters and events are the same. Think about how they are different.

Cousins in Space

The first day at Space Camp was busy. Tanya and Ashley both wore space suits. They climbed a zero-gravity wall wearing harnesses that held them up in the air. They felt as if they were floating in space. Tanya was excited, but Ashley felt a little sick. Later the girls built parts for a space station and exercised in a machine like a hamster's wheel.

"Aren't you glad we decided to come to Space Camp?" Tanya asked at dinner. "I loved the gravity chair that made me feel almost weightless."

"I guess so," Ashley said slowly. "I didn't like the chair, though. It made me really dizzy."

They chewed their dried space food. No one liked that very much.

The next day the girls flew an imaginary mission on a space shuttle.

Some campers acted as astronauts, while others remained on the ground to assist them. Tanya was an astronaut, and Ashley stayed on the ground. She guided the astronauts using a computer. She saved the space shuttle when it was in danger. The instructor told Ashley that she made good decisions. Tanya took off her helmet and saw that Ashley looked proud.

"Guess what?" Ashley said.

"I know—now you want to be an astronaut, just like me," Tanya said.

"Not exactly. We're both interested in space," said Ashley. "You want to be an astronaut. I want to work in mission control. We can be the first cousins in the space program. While you are up in space, I'll be on the ground assisting you. What a great way to work together!"

Checking Comprehension

Write the answer to each question on the lines.

1. How did the girls find ways they could both be happy in a space program?

   _____

   _____

2. Would you like to go to Space Camp? Why or why not?

   _____

   _____

Practicing Comprehension Skills

Read the sentences. Circle **compare** if the sentence tells how Tanya and Ashley are alike. Circle **contrast** if the sentence tells how Tanya and Ashley are different.

3. Tanya and Ashley both liked Space Camp.   **compare**   **contrast**

4. Tanya felt excited, but Ashley felt sick.   **compare**   **contrast**

Use the Venn diagram to compare and contrast Tanya and Ashley. Under Tanya's name, write two things that tell only about her. Under Ashley's name, write two things that tell only about her. In the middle, write two things that are true about both of them.

Tanya   **Both**   **Ashley**

5. _____   7. _____   9. _____

   _____   _____   _____

6. _____   8. _____   10. _____

   _____   _____   _____

STRATEGY: Comparing and Contrasting   **39**

11. Use the following chart to compare and contrast yourself with Tanya and Ashley.

I am most like _____ because _____ _____ _____ _____ .	I am least like _____ because _____ _____ _____ _____ .

Practicing Vocabulary

Choose the word from the box to complete each comparison.
Write the word on the line.

instructor	floating	danger	chewed	gravity	helmet	shuttle

12. Space is to weightlessness as Earth is to _____ .

13. Foot is to boot as head is to _____ .

14. Down is to sinking as up is to _____ .

15. Learn is to student as teach is to _____ .

16. Road is to car as sky is to _____ .

17. Milk is to sipped as sandwich is to _____ .

18. Harmless is to safety as harmful is to _____ .

Writing a Descriptive Paragraph
Write a paragraph that compares and contrasts Space Camp with a special place you have gone to. Tell how the two places are alike in some ways but different in other ways.

Summarizing

After you read a story or an article, it is a good idea to think about the most important ideas you want to remember. When you tell the main ideas of what you have read in your own words, you are **summarizing**.

A summary of a story tells the most important events that happened. A summary of an article tells the most important ideas. Summarizing is helpful when you want to remember what a story or an article is about or when you want to tell someone else about it.

Read this article about a popular sport. Think about the most important ideas you want to remember.

Basketball is one of the most popular sports in the United States today. This sport may be popular because it is simple, and it can be played almost anywhere. All that is needed is a basketball, a hoop, and a smooth, hard surface. Teams can play against each other, or two friends can play a game of one-on-one.

Many great athletes have played the game. As young people watch superstars like Shaquille O'Neal and Rebecca Lobo, they get excited. They want to learn the game and do their best to play like superstars, too.

Fill in the circle before the right answer.

What are these paragraphs mostly about?

○ basketball   ○ superstars   ○ games

Which ideas would you include in a summary of the article?

○ Basketball is simple and can be played almost anywhere.

○ You need a ball, a hoop, and a hard surface.

○ Many kids dream of playing like a superstar.

○ The game can be played with a team or a friend.

> **Tip**
>
> A summary is always shorter than the story or article you are telling about. When writing a summary use your own words to tell only the most important ideas.

THE MAN CALLED AIR

Famous basketball player Michael Jordan didn't even make his high school varsity basketball team. He kept working at basketball. It is said he would practice alone in the school gym early in the mornings. Throughout his career, he worked harder to become better and better.

Michael Jordan's hard work finally paid off. Today he is considered by most people to have been the best basketball player in the history of the game. He was nicknamed Air because he seemed to be almost airborne when he played. This means it looked like he could almost fly. He could jump higher, shoot better, and move quicker than any other player.

Michael Jordan was a leader on the court. With Jordan's leadership, the Chicago Bulls won the World Championship five times. In one game he scored 69 points!

Jordan retired from basketball in 1998. Basketball stars Larry Bird and Magic Johnson agree that there is no other player like Michael Jordan and there probably never will be. He is a favorite of fans and athletes all over the world.

Checking Comprehension

Write the answer to the question on the lines.

1. What did Michael Jordan do to help himself reach his goal?

    _____

    _____

2. Why do you think Michael Jordan is a favorite of fans and athletes
    around the world?

    _____

    _____

Practicing Comprehension Skills

3. What is this article mostly about? Fill in the circle.

    ○ basketball   ○ Michael Jordan

    ○ the Chicago Bulls   ○ the World Championship

4. What are the most important ideas of this article? Fill in the circles.

    ○ Michael Jordan worked hard   ○ He sometimes went to the gym
       to become a great athlete.   at six o'clock in the morning.

    ○ Jordan was nicknamed Air.   ○ He is considered one of the best
                                            basketball players ever.

    ○ He could jump higher, shoot   ○ Larry Bird and Magic Johnson are
       better, move quicker, and score   basketball stars, too.
       more points than almost anyone.

5. Use the ideas you chose in number 4 to write a summary.

    _____

    _____

    _____

Fill in the circle next to each correct answer.

6. When you write a summary of an article, what should you remember to do?

   ○ Find the most important ideas in the article.

   ○ Include only the details that interest you.

   ○ Write down only the important ideas in your own words.

   ○ Compare your summary with the article to be sure you included every important idea.

Practicing Vocabulary

Choose the word from the box that best replaces each underlined word or phrase. Write the word on the line.

airborne	career	championship	athletes	favorite	retired	varsity

_____ 7. Chocolate is my <u>best-liked</u> flavor of ice cream.

_____ 8. Michael Jordan's <u>job</u> was playing basketball.

_____ 9. Mr. Adams <u>gave up working</u> when he turned sixty-five.

_____ 10. Some ball players seem like they are <u>floating in air</u>.

_____ 11. Many children hope to be <u>players of sports</u> in high school.

_____ 12. Our <u>best players'</u> baseball team won ten games last fall.

_____ 13. At the end of the season, they won the state <u>contest that decided a final winner</u>.

Writing a Summary
Think about a chapter you read recently in a science or social studies book. What were the most important ideas you read? On another piece of paper, write a paragraph that summarizes the main ideas of the chapter.

Author's Purpose

An author writes for different reasons. The reason an author writes is called the **author's purpose**. Authors write for one or more of these purposes:

- to entertain readers by telling an interesting or funny story
- to inform readers by telling information or teaching something new
- to persuade readers to think a certain way
- to express feelings by describing a person, place, or experience

Thinking about the author's purpose helps you understand what you read.

Read each paragraph. Think about the author's purpose.

Paragraph 1

Carnival is a street festival with parades, music, and costumes. This celebration is usually held in March or April.

Paragraph 2

You can learn about a special festival. Just read the book *Carnival* by Catherine Chambers. Find out if Carnival is like a holiday you celebrate!

Paragraph 3

People wearing colorful masks and costumes danced to lively music. Floats passed by cheering crowds. Carnival had begun.

Paragraph 4

Rosa and Mateo heard drum music coming from the streets. They smelled saltfish cakes. They were excited because Carnival had begun!

Write the number of the paragraph next to the purpose you think the author had for writing.

_____ to persuade others to read a book

_____ to express feelings by describing a celebration

_____ to inform readers about a festival called Carnival

_____ to entertain by telling a story

Tip

Before you read an article or story, look at the title and pictures to help you predict what the author's purpose or purposes might be.

On Your Own Look at the title and picture. Think about what the author's purpose might be. Read the article to see if you are right.

Handmade Valentine Greetings

If you want to send a one-of-a-kind valentine greeting, don't go to the rack of greeting cards at the store. Instead, make your own valentine card. Here are three ideas.

♥ **Balloon Blasters** Write and draw your message on a small piece of paper. Then roll it up tightly, tie it with a thin ribbon, and put it inside a balloon. Blow up the balloon, tie it, and add a string. Deliver the balloon with the suggestion to have a blast.

♥ **Secret Messages** Cut a heart out of red construction paper so that it will fit on the front of a card made by folding another sheet of construction paper in half. Make up a code for your valentine message. The code might be numbers, letters, or shapes that stand for the letters of the alphabet. Write the key to the code on the back of the red heart before you glue it by one edge to the card cover. Fold back the heart to reveal the code.

♥ **Valentine Name Poems** To write a name poem, list the letters of your valentine's name in a column. Then write a description that begins with each letter.

These three ideas are just starting points. Use your own personal touches to make your cards special.

Checking Comprehension

Write the answer to each question on the lines.

1. Why might you want to make your own valentines?

   _____

2. How are the three valentine ideas in this article alike and different?

   _____

   _____

Practicing Comprehension Skills

Think about why the author wrote "Handmade Valentine Greetings." Put a check next to each statement you agree with.

_____ 3. The author wrote to tell a story about Valentine's Day.

_____ 4. The author explained how to write a name poem.

_____ 5. The author wanted to express feelings about getting valentine cards.

_____ 6. The author wanted to persuade readers to make handmade valentines.

_____ 7. The author wrote to inform readers about how to make personal valentine cards.

_____ 8. The author wanted to tell how Valentine's Day first started.

_____ 9. The author explained how to make a valentine using balloons.

Fill in the circles next to the right answers.

10. What details make you think the author wanted to give information?

    ○ The title tells me this.   ○ The art shows what I can make.

    ○ Directions are given to make three cards.   ○ A story is told.

11. What ideas does the author give to make you think about valentine cards in a different way?

○ Make cards instead of buying them. ○ Buy greeting cards.

○ Give gifts instead of cards. ○ Handmade valentines are special.

12. If the author wanted to entertain readers, what might the author write?

○ a play about Valentine's Day ○ a valentine mystery

○ a recipe for fudge ○ valentine riddles

Practicing Vocabulary

Choose a word from the box that best matches each clue.
Write the word on the line.

touches	poems	message	suggestion	description	code	valentine

_____ 13. an idea or thought

_____ 14. a person's own ways of doing things

_____ 15. writing that describes

_____ 16. symbols standing for the letters in words

_____ 17. a sweetheart or a card for a sweetheart

_____ 18. writings that express feelings, sometimes they rhyme

_____ 19. words sent from one person to another

Writing a Paragraph
On another piece of paper write a paragraph about a holiday. Your purpose can be to give information, express feelings, persuade others to celebrate, or tell a story. Share with a partner who can identify your purpose.

Statements of Fact/Opinion

When you read, you need to know the difference between statements of fact and statements that tell an author's opinion. A **statement of fact** tells something that can be proved true or false. You can check it by reading, observing, or asking an expert. A **statement of opinion** tells how a person feels, believes, or thinks. These statements cannot be proved true or false.

Statements of opinion may sound like facts because at first they seem to be true. It's important to know the difference when you are looking for information, because an opinion may change from one person to another, but facts do not change.

Read about the author E. B. White. Look for statements of fact and statements of opinion.

Have you ever read a book about a spider named Charlotte? Have you ever seen a movie about a mouse who is a member of a human family? Both stories were written by E. B. White.

E. B. White was born in Mount Vernon, New York, in 1899. He wrote many books for adults, but most people know him for his children's books—*Charlotte's Web, Stuart Little,* and *The Trumpet of the Swan.*

When E. B. White was a boy, he kept pigeons, lizards, turtles, and dogs as pets. Later he wrote stories about animals. Children today still love his stories. E. B. White will always be remembered as one of America's best writers for children.

Write **F** on the line for each statement of fact.
Write **O** for each statement of opinion.

_____ E. B. White will always be remembered as one of America's best writers for children.

_____ E. B. White was born in Mount Vernon, New York, in 1899.

_____ E. B. White wrote *Charlotte's Web, Stuart Little,* and *The Trumpet of the Swan.*

_____ Children today still love his stories.

Tip

Words that compare (*worst, best, sweetest*) and words that describe (*beautiful, silly, cute*) are clues that a statement is an opinion, since the statement of opinion cannot be proved true or false.

A student named Chris wrote a book report about E. B. White's book *Stuart Little*. As you read, look for statements of fact and statements of opinion.

STUART LITTLE

a book report by Chris Rush

As soon as Stuart Little is born, his parents realize that he is no ordinary son. He is only two inches tall and has a tail, two small ears, and whiskers. In fact, Stuart Little wouldn't be considered a boy at all—he's a mouse!

Stuart Little lives in an apartment in New York City with his two human parents. He has an older human brother who likes him and a cat named Snowbell who does not.

One day a sick bird named Margalo lands on Stuart's windowsill. Stuart's mother saves the bird and nurses it back to health. Stuart and Margalo become best friends.

I liked the character Stuart Little because he is very brave. He sails a boat on a pond by himself. When Snowbell almost eats Margalo, Stuart scares the cat away.

Stuart Little is a good friend, too. When Margalo disappears, Stuart is very upset. He leaves the house and searches for her.

I enjoyed this book because it made me laugh. It is about a character that I like. If Stuart Little lived next door to me, I would want to be his friend. The only thing I didn't like is that I never found out if Stuart went back home to his family. He wanted to, but then the book was suddenly over.

Even though I didn't like the ending, I would tell my friends to read this book. It is a book that all children can enjoy. They can read about friendship and bravery and laugh at the same time.

Checking Comprehension

Answer the questions. Write the answers on the lines.

1. Why do you think the writer would want to be Stuart Little's friend?

_____

_____

2. Do you think you would like to read this book? Tell your opinion. Explain why or why not.

_____

_____

Practicing Comprehension Skills

Read each statement about the book report.
Write **fact** or **opinion** next to each one.

_____ 3. A book about a mouse who acts like a boy is funny.

_____ 4. Stuart's mother saves the bird and nurses it back to health.

_____ 5. Stuart sails a boat in a pond.

_____ 6. Stuart Little is very brave.

_____ 7. Stuart and Margalo are friends.

_____ 8. The book's ending is not very good.

_____ 9. Stuart lives in an apartment.

_____ 10. Everyone would want to be Stuart's friend.

_____ 11. Stuart leaves home to search for Margalo.

_____ 12. *Stuart Little* is a book children can enjoy.

Write one statement of fact and one statement of opinion
about the book report on *Stuart Little*.

13. Statement of Fact

_____

_____

14. Statement of Opinion

_____

_____

Practicing Vocabulary

Write a word from the box to complete each sentence.

apartment	character	he's	ordinary	searches	whiskers	wouldn't

15. Stuart's family lives in an _____ .

16. The cat _____ under the bed for the mouse.

17. Something that happens every day is _____ .

18. Cats have _____ on their faces.

19. A mouse probably _____ be best friends with a bird.

20. Stuart is the main _____ in a book.

21. As you read about Stuart, you realize that _____ a special mouse.

Writing a Book Report

On another sheet of paper, write a book report to tell
others about a book you have read. Tell what you liked and
didn't like about the book. Include statements of fact and
statements of opinion.

Making Judgments

Have you ever formed an opinion about someone in a story? Maybe you liked or disliked the character. Have you ever felt as if an author was trying to get you to agree with an idea? Maybe you agreed, and maybe you didn't.

When you form opinions about characters and events, and when you agree or disagree with things that you read, you are **making judgments**. Making judgments means thinking about and deciding how you feel toward people, events, and ideas in stories and articles. Use what you know and what you have read to make judgments.

Read this article about wolves in the wild. Decide if you agree with what the author says.

Less than 100 years ago, wolves had disappeared from our western states. Wolves ate people's cattle and sheep. They were seen as dangerous killers.

Scientists who studied wolves did not think this way. The fact that wolves live and travel in packs made them interesting animals to study. Wolves were also useful in keeping down the number of elk and coyotes, helping to balance the food supply for other animals.

As time passed many people realized that the scientists were right. Laws were then passed to protect wolves. Beginning in 1994, wolves were captured in the far north and set free in Yellowstone National Park. Now the wolves have returned to the West!

What judgment about wolves can you make based on the article?

_____

What details does the author give to help you make a judgment about wolves?

_____

_____

_____

Tip

To decide if your judgment is fair, look again at what you have read and use details as proof to back up your judgment.

Read this story about wolves. Make judgments based on what you read.

A Safe New Home

The large female wolf ran, and the six wolves in the pack followed. She heard the *whirr whirr* of a huge bird and saw its shadow on the snow. She was trying to lead the pack to the safety of the trees across the field.

Soon the wolf could not run anymore, and she fell to the ground. She did not know about the dart in her side. It was filled with medicine to make her sleep.

When the wolf awoke, she was confused by the strange sounds and the darkness. Suddenly, she saw another wolf. It was her grown daughter! The two wolves greeted each other by licking and rubbing.

For a long, long time, the two wolves lay curled together in this dark place. The ground was rocking back and forth under them. The rocking motion stopped and suddenly sunlight appeared. Two strange creatures were standing before them. The wolves had never seen people before. The large wolf bared her teeth and growled at them.

For a short time the two wolves lived inside a fenced area. Meat was brought for them to eat, and they had each other for company. From inside the pen the wolves saw trees and snow, and they sniffed at the smells in the air. Soon they got used to this new place.

One spring day the strangers arrived to open the gate. The large wolf carefully went near the opening and then darted out. She called, and her daughter followed. They ran like the wind. They were free!

"May they have long and happy lives here in Yellowstone National Park!" said the hopeful voice of the park ranger.

Checking Comprehension

Write the answer to each question on the lines.

1. Who are the strangers and what are they doing with the wolves?

   _____

   _____

   _____

2. How does the wolf feel when she first sees the strange creatures? Why?

   _____

   _____

   _____

Practicing Comprehension Skills

Circle **YES** or **NO** after each statement below.
Use the lines to write a reason for your choice.

3. The wolves should have been taken from their home.　　**YES**　　**NO**

   _____

   _____

4. The wolves should be returned to their first home.　　**YES**　　**NO**

   _____

   _____

5. Wolves belong in Yellowstone National Park.　　**YES**　　**NO**

   _____

   _____

Answer each question. Write a reason for each judgment.

6. Do you believe that wolves have feelings?

Yes, because _____

No, because _____

7. Do you believe that wolves are smart?

Yes, because _____

No, because _____

8. Why should people care about wildlife?

_____

Practicing Vocabulary

Choose a word from the box that best matches each clue.
Write the word on the line.

| lives |
| motion |
| female |
| company |
| bared |
| wolves |
| sniffed |

_____ **9.** wild animals that look like dogs

_____ **10.** movement

_____ **11.** more than one life

_____ **12.** showed something, such as teeth

_____ **13.** someone to be with

_____ **14.** male wolf's partner

_____ **15.** used the nose

Writing a Poem
Think of an animal that you want people to care about.
On another piece of paper, write a poem to express what
makes the animal special and why it deserves concern.

LESSON 14

Paraphrasing

After you read an interesting article or story, do you ever share the details or information with others? You probably do. You tell about the writer's ideas, but you say them in your own way. You use different words than the author did, but you do not change the meaning of the story or article. Using your own words to tell about what you read is one way to make sure you understand and remember it.

Read the article below. Think about how you could use your own words to retell the information.

You probably know that it's important to wear a helmet when you ride a bike. Do you know the right way to wear a helmet, though? A bike helmet should fit snugly. It should move only one inch when you push it from front to back. Use sponge pads if you need to make the fit tighter.

Wear the helmet with its front above your eyebrows. The front and back straps should form a V just below your ear. Tighten the straps if the helmet is loose. Test the chin strap after buckling it. It should be snug when your mouth is open. If you wear your helmet correctly, it will help keep you safe.

Think about the important information you just read. Put a check by the sentences that have the same meaning as the article.

_____ It's probably a good idea to wear a bike helmet. Choose a helmet that looks good. It should fit snugly, too. The straps should form a V under each ear. Make sure your helmet is pushed back so you can see.

_____ Wear a helmet when you ride a bike. Your helmet should be snug and not move around. Add pads to make it fit. Straps should be tight and form a V below the ears. The front of the helmet should be just above your eyebrows.

Tip

As you retell what you have read, remember to keep the writer's meaning when you use your own words. Do not add any opinions.

PEDAL, TIMOTHY!

by Joyce Annette Barnes

"Pedal, Timothy!" Dee said. She was trotting along the sidewalk, holding onto her five-year-old brother's new two-wheel bicycle. Four years ago, Dee was Timothy's age, and she was the one learning to ride. Now it was Timothy's turn, and Dee was thrilled to be his teacher.

"Don't let go!" Timothy answered. He turned his head to make sure she was still there just as Dee let go of the bike.

Timothy wobbled, yelped, and fell down in a clatter. Dee had made sure he put on his safety helmet. Still, he howled as he lay on the cold sidewalk. "I can't do it!" he yelled.

"Yes, you can. Try harder to keep your balance. Watch the sidewalk ahead—don't keep turning around. *Keep pedaling,* Timothy! One time, it'll happen. I promise."

Timothy pushed his feet onto the pedals once more. With just a quick glance at his sister, he set off again.

"That's it," Dee told him encouragingly. "Keep pedaling." Then she released him, just as she had done fifty times before. She held her breath. He was five feet ahead of her, then ten feet, then fifteen. That was the farthest he'd ever gone!

The bike wobbled. Then Timothy caught hold of himself and looked straight ahead. The bicycle's wheels sailed forward smoothly. He was riding! When he pedaled right into a row of bushes and fell into their prickly branches, he didn't even cry.

Dee ran to help him up. A grin was spreading across his face. "I did it by myself!" he said.

"Great!" Dee said. "Now you need to learn how to use the brakes!"

Checking Comprehension

Write the answer to each question on the lines.

1. Why do you think Dee worked so hard to help her brother learn to ride a bike?

   _____

   _____

2. How does Timothy change from the beginning of the story to the end?

   _____

   _____

Practicing Comprehension Skills

Match the sentence on the left with the sentence on the right
that has the same meaning. Write the number on the line.

3. The wheels did not stay straight.

4. The bike dropped noisily
    with Timothy on it.

5. Dee let go of the bike.

6. Timothy held his body in balance.

_____ Dee released her hold on the bike.

_____ The tires wobbled.

_____ Timothy caught hold of himself.

_____ Timothy and the bike fell down
      in a clatter.

Choose the sentence that most closely matches the sentence
from the story. Fill in the circle.

7. One time, it'll happen, I promise.

    ○ You will be able to ride if you keep trying.

    ○ You will be able to ride one time before falling again.

8. With just a quick glance at his sister, he set off again.

    ○ Timothy looked at his sister, then rode away as fast as he could.

    ○ Before Timothy rode off, he gave his sister a fast little look.

9. Retell each part of the story in your own words. Fill in the diagram.

Beginning (Subject and Characters)

_____

Middle (Problem)

_____

_____

End (Solution)

_____

Practicing Vocabulary

Choose the word from the box to finish each sentence in Timothy's story.

| balance encouragingly farthest howled released smoothly spreading |

Timothy couldn't ride his bike _____ . He tried harder to

_____ his bike. Timothy _____ when he fell.

His sister spoke to him _____ . Suddenly, Dee

_____ the bike. A grin was _____ across

Timothy's face. This was the _____ he had gone. He was riding!

Writing a Log Entry
Write a log entry about an experience you have had. Share your writing with a partner. Ask your partner to use his or her own words to retell what you have written.

Point of View

There are two ways an author can decide to tell a story. The first way is to have a character tell the story. The character will use the words *I*, *me*, and *we* to tell what happens. This is called **first-person point of view**.

An author might also decide to have the story told by a speaker who is not a character in the story. The speaker uses the words *he, she, it,* and *they* to tell the story. This is called **third-person point of view**.

Read the following two passages. Think about who is telling the story in each passage.

Passage A

My pal Wes and I are sports nuts. We spend hours playing, watching, and talking about sports. One day we saw kids playing a game with unusual sticks.

"So what is this game?" I asked a player who was sitting on the bench.

A girl gave me a surprised look and said to me, "Anyone who knows about sports knows about field hockey!"

Passage B

Chris and Wes are sports nuts. They spend hours playing, watching, and talking about sports. One day they saw kids playing a game with unusual sticks.

"So what is this game?" Chris asked a player who was sitting on the bench.

A girl gave him a surprised look and said, "Anyone who knows about sports knows about field hockey!"

Fill in the chart. Write if the speaker is **a character** or **not a character**. Then write **first person** or **third person** under **Point of View**.

Passage	Speaker	Point of View
A	_____	_____
B	_____	_____

Tip

When you read, think about who is telling the story. Ask yourself how the story would be different from another point of view.

Soccer Star

My Day as a Forward

Jorge loved soccer, but he wasn't a very good player. His teammates teased him, and even the Comets' coach got frustrated with him. The coach told Jorge he needed more practice, especially with his footwork. Jorge practiced after school every day and on weekends. He watched games on TV to pick up tips. He asked his teammates for help.

Soon the coach began to notice Jorge's improvement. Finally all the hours of hard work paid off. The coach thought very carefully. He decided to take a chance on Jorge and make him a forward. Jorge was thrilled. This would put Jorge in a position to be a scorer for his team. Jorge helped his teammates win the game that day. He proved to everyone that he could play well not just in practice, but in a real game!

I loved soccer, but I wasn't a very good player. My teammates teased me, and my coach got frustrated with me. My coach told me I needed more practice, especially on my footwork. I practiced after school every day and on weekends. I watched games on TV to pick up tips. I even asked my teammates for help. I hoped my coach noticed some improvement.

The day of our big game, I felt a tap on my shoulder as I sat on the bench. I looked up and saw my coach.

"OK, Jorge, you go in as a forward," he said to me.

I was thrilled. Finally all those hours of hard work would pay off. I helped my teammates win the game that day. I proved to them that I could play well not just in practice, but in a real game!

Checking Comprehension

Write the answer to each question on the lines.

1. Why did the coach make Jorge a forward?

_____

_____

2. Do you think Jorge will be selected to play forward in future games? Explain your answer.

_____

_____

Practicing Comprehension Skills

Use what you have learned about point of view to answer each question. Fill in the circle next to your answer.

3. Who is telling the story "Soccer Star"?
   ○ a character in the story   ○ not a character in the story

4. From what point of view is this story told?
   ○ first-person point of view   ○ third-person point of view

5. What words help you know which point of view is used?
   ○ the words *I* and *me*   ○ the words *he* and *his*

6. Who is telling the story "My Day As a Forward"?
   ○ a character in the story   ○ not a character in the story

7. From what point of view is this story told?
   ○ first-person point of view   ○ third-person point of view

8. What words help you know which point of view is used?
   ○ the words *I* and *me*   ○ the words *he* and *his*

Rewrite these sentences from Jorge's point of view.

9. The coach told Jorge he needed more practice.

   _____

10. He asked his teammates for help.

    _____

Rewrite this sentence from a third-person point of view.

11. I looked up and saw my coach.

    _____

Practicing Vocabulary

Choose the word from the box that matches each definition.
Write the word on the line.

teammates	improvement	position	scorer	practice	forward	hard

_____ 12. a group of players on a team

_____ 13. do something over and over again

_____ 14. becoming better

_____ 15. one who makes a point for a team

_____ 16. difficult

_____ 17. position on a soccer team

_____ 18. a place for a player

Writing a Narrative Paragraph
Write about a sports event you have experienced. Use first-person point of view to tell your story. Remember to use words like *I, me,* and *we.*

Text Structure

Authors try to give information in a clear and organized way. When you read writing that gives information about something, look for how the details are organized. The author may tell how things are alike and different. The author may tell what happens first, next, and last in a story. The author may also explain causes and effects. Different kinds of information are organized in different ways.

Read the following article. Think about how the information is organized.

Look up! Kites of all kinds are soaring. Each kite is made of a lightweight frame and a covering. Each one is connected to the ground by a long cord. Do you see some differences?

The most common types of kites used are the flat kite and the box kite. One popular flat kite is known as the diamond kite. Like all flat kites, it has to have a tail to stay balanced. Box kites balance more steadily in changing winds than flat kites do. However, they do not usually rise as high.

Underline the most important ideas about kites.

Kites need to be lightweight with a cord.

Kites soar gracefully like birds.

Box kites are steadier than flat kites.

Flat kites rise higher than box kites.

Underline the way the writer organized the information about kites.

cause and effect

likenesses and differences

what happens first, next, and last

Tip

When you read, notice how the information is organized. This can help you understand and remember it better.

Read the article. Think about how facts and ideas are organized.

Kites Of Long Ago

Nobody knows when or where kite flying began, but there are some clues about the history of kites. Early kites may have been simple flat shapes such as leaves. Later, kite designs improved as people discovered how to put lightweight coverings over frames. Silk and paper are lightweight materials that were invented in China. China is the earliest known center of kite making. Chinese kites date back at least 2,000 years.

The first Chinese kites may have been used by armies, perhaps as signals. As time passed, kites took on other uses. They were flown during special ceremonies and for sport. Then there were kite-flying holidays, such as the one held on the ninth day of the ninth month. According to legend, that was the day a family went kite-flying on a hilltop. Returning to their house, they saw that it had collapsed. Kite-flying had saved their lives!

After a while, travelers and traders spread kite-flying from China to Japan. Before long, Japanese kite-flying took on a new purpose. Kites flew to celebrate happy occasions and to bring a favorable future. Soon, kite-flying reached many other Asian countries. In each land, remarkable kites were designed for ceremonies and sport.

Later, knowledge of kites traveled west, to northern Africa, to Europe, and finally to the Americas. There may have been early kite inventors in these lands, but their creations did not spread as widely as the kites of Asia.

Checking Comprehension

Write the answer to each question on the lines.

1. What clues tell you that the earliest kites were made in China?

   _____

   _____

2. What have kites been used for?

   _____

Practicing Comprehension Skills

Answer each question about the article. Fill in the correct circle.

3. How does the writer organize information about kites?

   ○ The writer uses sequence of events.

   ○ The writer lists problems and solutions.

   ○ The writer tells how things are alike and different.

   ○ The writer gives steps to tell how to do something.

4. Which set of words from the article helps you understand the writer's organization?

   ○ armies, signals, holidays

   ○ house, collapsed, kite-flying

   ○ Asia, China, Japan

   ○ at first, after a while, later

5. Write these words to show how kites were used from early times to today.

ceremonies	happy occasions	armies	sport

1. _____	→	2. _____	→	3. _____	→	4. _____

6. Show where kite flying was used from the first place to the last.

Asia Japan China Europe Africa Americas

1. _____	→	2. _____	→	3. _____

↓

6. _____	←	5. _____	←	4. _____

Practicing Vocabulary

Choose the word from the box that best matches
each meaning. Write the word on the line.

designs remarkable ceremonies favorable creations celebrate improved

_____ **7.** to have a party

_____ **8.** made better

_____ **9.** good

_____ **10.** worth noting

_____ **11.** things that have been made

_____ **12.** plans or drawings to use as a pattern

_____ **13.** actions performed for a special occasion

Writing an Informative Paragraph
On another piece of paper, write a paragraph about
something that flies. Decide how you will organize your
details. You can make comparisons, use sequence, or
explain causes and effects.

Author's Viewpoint

Every author writes about people and things in his or her own special way. The way an author looks at the subject or ideas he or she is writing about is called the **author's viewpoint**.

To find out what an author thinks, feels, or believes, you must look at the words the author uses and the opinions he or she shares. Words like *most amazing*, *wonderful*, *important*, and *exciting* will give you a good idea of how the author feels about the subject. You have a viewpoint, too. You may or may not think and feel the same way that the author does.

Read the passage. Decide what the author thinks and feels about the Fossil Halls.

The American Museum of Natural History in New York City is the world's largest natural history museum. This exciting museum has one of the most important collections of dinosaurs and fossils in the world. Some of the most amazing exhibits are found in the six Fossil Halls.

You will enjoy the way the Fossil Halls tell the story of how animals with backbones developed and changed. There are more than 600 wonderful examples of fossils to see. You can learn about the fossils in several different ways. You might have the most fun using the computers.

Put an X before the sentence that best tells the author's viewpoint about the Fossil Halls.

_____ The Fossil Halls give too much information.

_____ The Fossil Halls are an amazing and exciting place to learn.

_____ The Fossil Halls are not as interesting as some other parts of the museum.

Tip

When you read, ask yourself, "What does the author think or believe about this person, thing, or idea? What words does the author use that are clues to how he or she feels?"

On Your Own

Read this story. Decide what the author thinks, feels, and believes about fossils.

FOSSILS
Tell Amazing Stories

by J. Lynett Gillette

We were high in the Utah mountains in a squishy, wet bog when we found the fossil. It was the cheekbone of a mammoth, a kind of elephant that is now extinct. As our group dug in the mud, we began to see a whole mammoth skeleton.

As a paleontologist, a scientist who studies fossils, I was thrilled to see remains that were so well preserved. The cold temperature had worked like a deep freezer. Usually Ice Age fossil bones are easily broken. These bones seemed so fresh that we could still bend the ribs. We discovered mammoth dung, too. It was full of needles of fir and spruce trees. Now we knew that the mammoth had eaten very poorly in its last days.

Back in the lab we looked at mud from the bog. Under the microscopes we saw a few bits of pollen from grasses that make tiny flowers only in the spring. We knew that the mammoth had died in springtime. It was an old male. He had broken his leg at the time he died. We all began to feel very kindly toward the grand old beast. His last day seemed very real to us. Perhaps he struggled as he was stuck in the bog.

Weeks later we heard a rumor that stone arrowheads had been found close to the dig site. We didn't know exactly where they were found, because someone had slipped the little treasures into a pocket. The thief had robbed us all. We would never learn if prehistoric hunters had killed our mammoth.

Checking Comprehension

1. What did you learn about the mammoth from reading the passage?

_____

_____

2. Why do you think the paleontologists were so excited to find mammoth bones?

_____

_____

Practicing Comprehension Skills

Read each group of sentences. Check the sentence that best tells the author's viewpoint. Then give a reason for your choice.

3. ____ The author thinks fossils are precious because they tell about the past.

   ____ The author thinks fossils are too easy to find.

   ____ The author thinks a paleontologist is the most important scientist.

   Why do you think this is true?

   _____

   _____

4. ____ The author thinks mammoth bones are the most important fossils.

   ____ The author thinks it is wrong to take fossils or other items from dig sites.

   ____ The author thinks the mammoth was killed by hunters.

   Why do you think this is true?

   _____

   _____

STRATEGY: Understanding Author's Viewpoint 71

5. Find words in the passage that show how the author feels about the following things. Write the words below.

fossils _____

the mammoth _____

the thief _____

6. Would you feel the same way about finding fossils?　　**YES**　　**NO**
Explain your answer.

_____

_____

Practicing Vocabulary

Write a word from the box to finish each sentence in this journal entry.

beast　fossil　freezer　paleontologist　prehistoric　skeleton　temperature

Today I worked with a _____ to look for dinosaur bones from

_____ times. We found a bone from the _____

of an apatosaurus. This huge _____ lived 150 million years ago. We

also found a _____ of an early relative of a frog. The fossil and the

bone must be stored at a very cold _____ . When we got back to

her office, we put them in a special _____ .

Writing a Journal Entry
Write a journal entry to tell about a school event. Express your viewpoint of what happened and how you felt about this event. Compare and contrast your writing with a partner's viewpoint of the same event.

Making Generalizations

Sometimes when you read, you are given ideas about a group of people, animals, or things. You can use what you have read and what you already know to make a statement about them as a group. This statement might tell how they are alike or mostly alike in some way. Making statements like this can help you understand more about what you read. It can also help you explain what you read to someone else.

Read this passage. Think about a statement you might make about cats as a group.

When someone says *cat*, you probably think of a little furry pet that meows and cuddles up to you. Now think of a cat that is nine feet long, has a three-foot long tail, and weighs 600 pounds! Yes, tigers are cats, too. Besides the house cat and the tiger, the cat family includes jaguars, leopards, lions, cheetahs, pumas, and lynx. You'll find that cats live in almost every part of the world. Different kinds of cats can be from 20 inches to 9 feet long, without counting that long tail. A house cat usually weighs about 10 pounds. You already know what the tiger weighs!

Fill in the circle next to each statement that is true about cats.

○ Most cats are cuddly.

○ There are many different kinds of cats in the cat family.

○ Cats come in many different sizes from small to very large.

Fill in the circles next to the details that prove the statements you chose above.

○ Most cats can be from 20 inches to 9 feet long.

○ A tiger's tail can be three feet long.

○ The cat family includes house cats, tigers, jaguars, leopards, lions, cheetahs, pumas, and lynx.

Tip

When you read about a group of animals, people, or things, ask yourself: How are all of them alike? What can I say about them as a group? Making a statement to answer these questions will help you remember what you read.

STRATEGY: Making Generalizations 73

KING of the APES

Imagine an animal that is six feet tall and weighs 450 pounds. Imagine an animal with long, sharp teeth and huge jaws. Imagine an animal that can bend a rubber car tire in half. This animal is not make-believe. It is a gorilla, the most powerful ape of all.

Gorillas look frightening and may seem dangerous, but they are really gentle, shy creatures who hardly ever fight. They eat bamboo shoots and wild celery, not other animals. They like to eat, sleep, and play with their babies. They also like to groom each other. They look at each other's fur and take out insects and dirt. These huge animals actually live quite peaceful lives.

Gorillas like to spend time with other gorillas. They live in groups called troops, which usually include 10 to 15 gorillas. The leader of the troop is a large, older male that has silver hair on its back. He is called a silverback. A troop also has females, their babies, and a few young males.

Gorillas travel together looking for food. They travel on the ground, walking on their feet and on the knuckles of their hands. The silverback decides where they will go. If he sees danger, he roars and slaps his chest, causing other animals to get scared and run away. At night the gorillas make nests of leaves and grass. They sleep in trees or on the ground.

Gorillas are not only strong, they are also very smart. They learn quickly. In fact, one famous gorilla has even learned to talk to people by using sign language!

Checking Comprehension

1. Why might people be scared if they came face to face with a gorilla?

_____

_____

2. What qualities do all gorillas have?

_____

_____

Practicing Comprehension Skills

Put a check next to the statement you believe to be true
after reading "King of the Apes."

_____ 3. Huge animals that look frightening are dangerous.

_____ 4. Gorillas are animals that need to live together in a community.

_____ 5. All animals live in troops with a leader.

Put a check next to each fact that proves this statement to be true.

_____ 6. Gorillas live in groups called troops.

_____ 7. Gorillas eat, sleep, and play with their babies.

_____ 8. Gorillas groom each other.

_____ 9. Gorillas eat plants.

_____ 10. Gorillas travel together looking for food.

_____ 11. One famous gorilla learned sign language.

Read this statement about gorillas: **Gorillas are smart animals.**

12. What details from the article make you think this is true?

_____

13. Finish this sentence to make another statement about gorillas.

Gorillas are _____ animals.

○ peaceful   ○ violent   ○ lazy   ○ angry

What details from the article helped you to decide this?

_____

_____

Practicing Vocabulary

Write a word from the box that belongs in each group.

frightening	groom	knuckles	dangerous	silverback	troop	peaceful

_____ **14.** not safe, risky

_____ **15.** leader, older male gorilla

_____ **16.** scary, terrifying

_____ **17.** take care of, make clean

_____ **18.** quiet, calm

_____ **19.** group, herd

_____ **20.** hands, fingers

Writing an Informative Paragraph
On another sheet of paper, write a paragraph about an interesting animal group. Make statements that tell how the animals in this group are alike or mostly alike in some way.

Literary Elements: Character

Characters are the people or animals in a story. When you read a story, pay close attention to the details about each character. Authors help you get to know their story characters by describing them, by telling what each character says and does, and by the thoughts or comments of other characters. Characters may remind you of people you know. They may even remind you of yourself.

Read the story about a girl's first visit to the ocean. Think about the character named Mara.

On Mara's first visit to the ocean, her father held her hand as the chilly water tickled her feet. "I want to go in!" Mara said immediately. They waded in to meet the waves, and Mara's heart soared.

Afterward, Mara strolled along the sand. "What animal lived in this shell?" she asked her father. "And what about this shell, and this one?" Looking down, she picked up a green stringy-looking substance. "What is this, Dad? Is it a plant or an animal?"

Her father laughed, "You really enjoy learning about new things, don't you?"

When they got home, Mara found some books about the ocean and began reading. She had a new dream. She wanted to dive underwater someday.

Fill in the circle before the word that describes Mara.

○ fearful   ○ curious   ○ mean   ○ shy

What does Mara do or say to make you think this way?

_____

_____

_____

Tip

Try to understand what story characters are like. The better you know them, the more you will understand and enjoy the story.

Read the poem. Think about the main character, Augie McNaughton.

The Dreamer

by J. Patrick Lewis

As Augie McNaughton got ready for school,
A full moon caught his eye.
He stared at it far too long, and soon
The school bus passed him by.

Then Augie McNaughton ran to school
(Arriving at half past eight),
And he told his teacher, Mrs. O'Toole,
That the moon had made him late.

She gave him a book with a knowing look
And said, "You will be amazed!"
As he read *The Skies Above,* he dreamed
In an Augie McNaughton haze.

When Augie McNaughton returned from school,
Aunt Maude asked what he'd been taught.
"I learned about space," Augie said. "Can you picture
Me as an astronaut?"

And awesome Augie grew and grew
With a faraway look in his eyes. . . .
I saw him once in a rocket ship
That soared across the skies.

Checking Comprehension

Write the answer to each question on the lines.

1. Why is this poem called "The Dreamer"?

   _____

   _____

2. Do you think Augie's dream came true? How can you tell?

   _____

   _____

Practicing Comprehension Skills

3. What kind of character is Augie? Write one or more words in each circle to describe him.

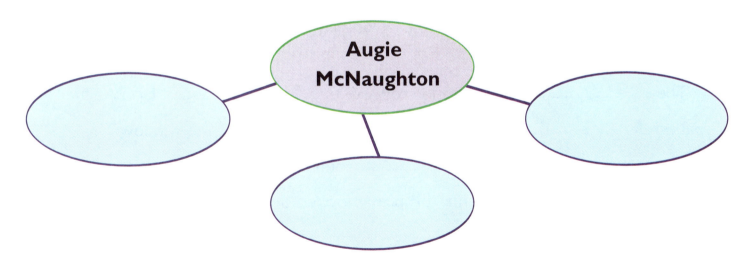

Read each question. Fill in the circle next to the correct answer.

4. What does Augie do to show that he is a dreamer?

   ○ He stares at the moon and misses the bus.

   ○ He is late for school.

   ○ He runs to school.

   ○ He gets ready for school.

5. What can you tell about Augie from the way he stares at the moon?

○ He doesn't like school.

○ He doesn't like the moon.

○ He sometimes walks to school.

○ He's amazed by the moon.

6. What does Augie mean by, "Can you picture me as an astronaut?"

○ His aunt is interested in space.

○ He dreams of traveling in space.

○ He drew a picture of an astronaut.

○ He wants to read more about the moon.

7. Are you like Augie in any way? Explain how you are alike.

_____

_____

Practicing Vocabulary

Write a word from the box to finish the sentences in the following paragraph.

amazed	astronaut	awesome	faraway	haze	soared	stared

The _____ traveled toward _____ Mars. As the

spacecraft _____, he _____ out the window. The

astronaut noticed a _____ surrounding Earth. He was

_____ at how small his planet looked. Seeing Earth from outer space

was an _____ sight!

Writing a Character Sketch
Imagine a character who wants to explore a volcano, a jungle, the sea, space, or some other place. On another sheet of paper, describe your character. Include details to show what your character does and says.

Literary Elements: Plot

Every story has important things that happen at the beginning, in the middle, and at the end. These important things are called **main events**. The beginning of a story usually introduces the characters and setting. You begin to learn about a problem. The middle of the story gives more details and tells about how characters try to solve the problem. The end of the story tells you how everything works out. These important parts of a story and why they happen are called the **plot**.

Read the story about Fox and Crow. Look for the important events.

One day Crow held a huge chunk of cheese in her mouth. Fox walked by and looked up. His mouth began to water, so he thought of a plan to get Crow's cheese.

Fox said, "Hello, Crow! How gorgeous you look today! I've never seen a crow with such beautiful wings."

Crow said nothing, because she did not want to drop the cheese.

"If you would sing, you would be even more beautiful!" Fox added.

No one had ever said such nice things about Crow. So she forgot about the cheese and opened her mouth to sing the only song she knew. "Caw! Caw! Caw!"

As Crow cried out, the cheese fell from her beak. Before it hit the ground, Fox had gobbled it up. That's how Crow learned not to be tricked by someone who flattered her.

Circle the most important events.

Fox sees Crow with cheese.

Fox flatters Crow.

Crow says nothing.

Crow sings and drops the cheese.

Crow learns a lesson.

Tip

Sometimes, thinking about the order in which events happen will help you remember the plot of a story.

Read this story about Ben Hooper. Think about the important events that happen in the beginning, middle, and end of the story.

When Wishes Come True!

Ben Hooper wanted a pet of his own. So he thought about a way to earn money to buy a pet. Ben loved to paint, so he decided to earn money by painting signs.

One day after school, Ben saw Mrs. Flavors. She owned the local ice-cream store and needed a new sign. Ben created a wonderful sign with a five-scoop cone. Mrs. Flavors was very happy and paid Ben.

A few days later Ben got a call from Mrs. Flavors to come to the store.

When Ben arrived he couldn't believe his eyes. The ice cream he had painted had become real and had melted. The ground was covered with ants that were licking up the ice cream.

"I can't have this!" said Mrs. Flavors. "You won't work for me again!"

Ben's next job was with the Seashore Snack Shack. The owner wanted a beach scene painted on the walls inside the shop.

"Perfect!" said Mr. C. Shore as he paid Ben. The next day, Mr. C. Shore called and sounded annoyed. "Sand from your beach is blowing everywhere. My customers are complaining about the sand in their sandwiches. You won't work for me again!"

After more painting disasters, no one would hire Ben. He carefully checked the cans of paint and brushes he had been using. They all seemed ordinary. Then Ben got an idea.

"If everything I paint turns real," he thought, "then I'll paint what I wish for."

He carried his paints outdoors and went to work on the pavement. He painted a picture of the large collie dog he had always wanted.

"Why stop now?" he thought to himself. He painted striped cats and white rabbits. He painted turquoise parrots, giant-sized iguanas, and a spotted pony. Before long Ben was surrounded by many live pets.

Now, whenever Ben hears someone making a wish, he tells them, "Be careful what you wish for. Your wish might come true!"

Checking Comprehension

Write the answer to the question on the lines.

1. Why were the customers unhappy with Ben's painting?

   _____

   _____

2. What lesson does Ben learn?

   _____

   _____

Practicing Comprehension Skills

Read each story event listed below. If it is an important event, write **Yes** on the line in front of it. If it is not important, write **No**.

3. _____ Ben takes a job as a painter to earn money for a pet.

4. _____ Mrs. Flavors paid Ben.

5. _____ Mr. C. Shore owns the Seashore Snack Shack.

6. _____ Ben finishes the Seashore job in no time.

7. _____ Ben's paintings become real and cause many problems.

8. _____ Ben paints a picture of what he wishes for.

9. _____ Ben paints on pavement.

10. _____ Ben paints turquoise parrots.

11. _____ Ben learns a lesson about what happens when you get exactly what you wish for.

12. Write the important events to finish the story map.

| Beginning | _____ |

↓

| Middle | _____ |
| | _____ |

↓

| End | _____ |

Practicing Vocabulary

Write words from the box to finish the sentences in the following letter.

Dear Ben,

   I heard about your painting _____ . Some

store owners were _____ . They were

_____ because your paintings caused problems.

I _____ you are a very special painter. I saw your

painting on the _____ . The _____

parrots were great! I like to be _____ by

beautiful things. Will you paint a garden for me?

> disasters
> turquoise
> complaining
> pavement
> surrounded
> believe
> annoyed

                Your friend and neighbor,
                Mr. Buzz Bees

Writing a Story
On another piece of paper, write a short story about a lesson you have learned. Be sure to include a beginning, a middle, and an end.

Literary Elements: Setting

Where and when a story takes place is called the **setting**. The place where a story happens can be a real or make-believe place. The time when a story takes place might be many years ago. Other stories might tell about events that are happening now or events that could happen in the future.

Sometimes an author tells you the story's setting. Other times you have to look for details to figure it out. As you read, think about why a setting is important for the characters and events.

Read the story. Think about when and where the story takes place.

Jess is spending the summer with Aunt Minnie and Uncle Frank. It took two days on a railroad train to get to their home. Aunt Minnie and Uncle Frank have a two-story house with a grand staircase inside. Jess has his very own bedroom on the second floor.

As Jess looks down from the windows of his room, he notices crowds of busy people rushing in and out the many houses and shops that line the street. The clatter of the horses as they pull the fancy carriages never stops. This visit will be quite an exciting adventure for a boy from the prairie!

What is the setting of this story? Fill in the circle.

○ a house on the prairie long ago

○ a house on the prairie today

○ a house in the city long ago

○ a city in the future

What words or phrases gave you clues that helped you figure out the setting?

_____

_____

Tip

As you read a story, picture the setting in your mind. Think about how the story would change if events happened in a different time and place.

On Your Own Read what happens to a boy and his sister one day. Think about why the setting is so important to the characters and events.

Uncle Randolph's
TIME MACHINE

My brother Sean and I went to visit Uncle Randolph on his farm. Our uncle was constantly experimenting with things. We knew he'd been working on something in his barn.

On the second morning of our visit, we snuck out of the house before sunrise and took a peek in the barn. At first, everything looked normal. Bessie the cow was in her pen, the chickens were in their coop, and hay was scattered all around. Suddenly, in the corner, we noticed a huge metal machine with the words TIME MACHINE painted on it. We exchanged puzzled glances, and then smiled at each other.

Sean and I stepped inside the machine. As Sean closed the door, I pushed a button. The machine bumped and grumbled. "Watch the time. Don't stay too long!" a voice said.

Quickly, we pushed the door back open, but as we looked around in disbelief, we realized we weren't in Uncle Randolph's barn anymore. The wooden stalls and pens were replaced with what looked like see-through plastic. There was a team of robots milking cows, raking hay, and gathering eggs.

I asked, "Where's Uncle Randolph?" A robot answered, "Unable to compute Uncle Randolph. We do have an Uncle Sean." Sean wasn't prepared for that.

Then we went to the barn doors and peered outside. A flying saucer landed, and a robot stepped out to announce, "Shuttle for Mars. All aboard!"

Just then we heard a message coming from the time machine. It said, "You'd better hurry. Your time will be up soon."

We hurriedly returned to the machine, and five minutes later, we were back in Uncle Randolph's barn. As Sean and I looked at each other, we both said, "There's no place like home!"

Checking Comprehension

Answer the questions. Write the answers on the lines.

1. How can you tell that the time machine really worked?

_____

_____

2. Where did the brother and sister go in the time machine?

_____

_____

Practicing Comprehension Skills

Read each question. Fill in the circle next to all of the correct answers.

3. Which words best describe the setting at the beginning of this story?

   ○ a farm in the present   ○ a farm in the future

   ○ a farm in the past   ○ a city apartment in the present

4. Which of the following are clues to the setting at the beginning of the story?

   ○ Uncle Randolph's farm   ○ a time machine

   ○ chickens in a coop   ○ a cow in her pen

5. What words best describe the setting in the middle of the story?

   ○ in a house in the future   ○ inside a barn in the past

   ○ inside a barn in the future   ○ near a river in the future

6. Which of the following are clues to the second setting?

   ○ There was a shuttle to Mars.   ○ Sean is an older adult.

   ○ Cows are inside the barn.   ○ Robots are doing the work.

7. What story clues let you know that the Time Machine brought the characters back to the present?

_____

_____

8. How would the story be different if the setting remained inside a barn in the future?

_____

_____

Practicing Vocabulary

Choose a word from the box to match each definition.

unable	disbelief	normal	peered	experimenting	constantly	compute

_____ **9.** not able

_____ **10.** like most others or usual

_____ **11.** not believing

_____ **12.** looked around

_____ **13.** trying things out

_____ **14.** make sense

_____ **15.** all the time

Write a Description of a Setting
On another piece of paper write a description of your favorite place. This place might be the seashore, a movie theater, a barnyard, or your bedroom. Then draw a picture to show what your setting looks like.

Literary Elements: Theme

Every story always has one big idea that the author wants you to understand. In some stories, the big idea is a lesson about life. Maybe the author wants you to understand that friends are important or that practice makes perfect. Sometimes the author tells you what the big idea is, but not always. When you read a story, think about what the characters learn. Ask yourself, What does the author want me to know from this story? Your answer may be the big idea.

Read the story about Bear. See if you can figure out what the author wants you to understand.

Bear listened quietly to the bird's song. It was so lovely that he decided to capture the bird so he could hear its music all the time. In the bush there were two birds. One was plain, with dull brown feathers, but the other's orange feathers were as bright as sunshine!

"The beautiful one must be the singer!" said Bear. He snatched it, but the beautiful bird did not sing. It squawked so harshly that Bear let it go. From the safety of a treetop, the plain brown bird sang a song that was as sweet as honey.

Fill in the circle next to the sentence that best tells the big idea of the story.

○ You can't always judge something by the way it looks.

○ Treat others as you wish to be treated.

○ Beauty on the outside means beauty on the inside.

○ Birds can make beautiful music.

What details helped you choose your answer?

_____

_____

_____

> **Tip**
>
> Every story always has one big idea the author wants you to know. Sometimes what you already know can also help you understand a story's big idea.

Jake's Haircut

by Robin Pulver

"Oh, no!" Jake said. "My hair! I can't go to school tomorrow. I can't face my friends with this big bare spot showing!"

Mom frowned at her new barber shears. "I'm sorry, Jake. I should have practiced before I tried these out. It's a good thing hair grows back."

To make this horrible day worse, Jake's dog, Cal, was sick. Jake's father took him to visit the veterinarian, and Cal had to stay overnight.

Jake slept restlessly that night. He missed his dog. Cal always listened to Jake's problems.

On his way to school the next day, Jake saw his neighbor, Martha. "What did you do to your hair?" she asked, staring.

"Nothing," said Jake, struggling to be polite. He hurried to catch up with his friends Anna and Tomas, and told them about Cal.

"Cal's a great dog," they said. "He has to get better." They didn't mention Jake's hair. Real friends care about the way you feel inside, Jake thought, not the way you look on the outside.

When Jake got home from school, Mom was smiling. "Terrific news," she said. "Guess who's better?"

"Cal!" Jake shouted. "Is he home?" Just then, Cal came up and licked Jake's hand.

Jake hugged his dog. "Cal, what happened to *your* hair?" he asked.

"The vet had to shave that spot to give him a shot," Mom said.

Jake laughed. "As long as he's OK, he's still the same old Cal. Anyway, hair grows back!"

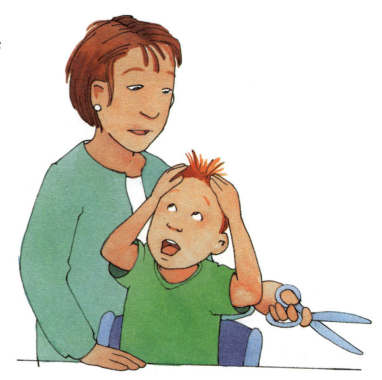

Checking Comprehension

Write the answer to each question on the lines.

1. What are Jake's two problems in the story?

   _____

   _____

2. How are Jake and Cal alike at the end of the story?

   _____

   _____

Practicing Comprehension Skills

Write the answer to the question on the lines.

3. What did you discover about friendship from reading this story?

   _____

   _____

Read each story detail. Write X next to details that have to do with the big idea of the story.

_____ 4. Jake's dog is named Cal.

_____ 5. Jake is afraid to face his friends.

_____ 6. Martha stares at Jake.

_____ 7. Cal had to be taken to the veterinarian.

_____ 8. Jake's friends do not mention his hair.

_____ 9. Cal licks Jake's hand.

_____ 10. Jake decides that hair grows back.

_____ 11. Cal had to be given a shot.

Fill in the circle next to the correct answer.

12. **What is the big idea the writer wants you to know from reading this story?**

○ Friends aren't always polite when you do something different.

○ How you look is not as important as who you are and how you feel.

○ Everyone should have real friends.

○ Pets sometimes get sick.

13. **What does the big idea make you think about?**

_____

_____

Practicing Vocabulary

Write a word from the box to finish each sentence.

listened	veterinarian	mention	frowned	restlessly	polite	visit

14. The _____ examined the sick cat.

15. The students _____ to their teacher.

16. They didn't _____ that Cora's socks did not match.

17. Bad dreams can make people sleep _____ .

18. Mom _____ at the mess in the kitchen.

19. It is _____ to say "please" and "thank you."

20. You should _____ the dentist once a year.

MAKING THE Reading AND Writing CONNECTION

Writing a Story
Write a story that has a big idea. Your big idea could be that friends share, celebrations bring joy to everyone, hard work pays off, or another idea. Share your story with a partner and ask him or her to tell what your big idea is.

Synonyms

Your friend says, "Get ready for a huge storm!" You say, "Get ready for a gigantic storm!" You are really both saying the same thing because *huge* and *gigantic* are **synonyms**. Synonyms are words that have the same or almost the same meaning. Knowing synonyms will help you understand difficult words when you read and help you choose the best words when you write.

Read the article. As you read, decide which words have the same or almost the same meaning.

It is a quiet day, the leaves are still, and even the birds are silent. White clouds float peacefully across the calm sky. Then, slowly at first, dark clouds begin to drift overhead. Suddenly, a flash of lightning crosses the sky. Should you go inside? Is a storm nearby?

Try this the next time you see lightning: Count seconds until you hear thunder. If five seconds go by, the storm is one mile away. If 10 seconds pass, it is two miles. What if only a second passes? The storm is approaching, and it is very CLOSE.

Think about the synonyms used in the story. Write a word from the box that is a synonym for each word below.

silent	calm	nearby	float

drift _____   quiet _____

still _____   close _____

Tip

To decide if a word is a synonym for another word, ask yourself if the word has the same or almost the same meaning.

On Your Own

Read the article. Think of synonyms that can be used in place of some words.

BELIEVE·IT·OR·NOT WEATHER TALES

Today if you want to know about the weather, you can switch on the radio or TV or go on-line and listen to a weather forecast. Long ago, when European settlers discovered a new life in America, there were no radios, no TVs, no computer — and no weather forecasters. So how did people know whether it would rain or snow? How did they predict the weather?

Folk tales, or sayings retold from generation to generation, helped early Americans forecast the weather. Many of these sayings sound unbelievable, and yet some of them have proven to be true, even today. Here are a few such examples:

Red sky in the morning, take warning.
Red sky at night, tomorrow's delight.
Red sky at noon, rain very soon.

High clouds bring good weather.
Seagulls sitting in the sand mean
*   that rain is surely at hand.*
Ground smells. Rain it tells.

Some early Americans also paid attention to animals and insects to help them predict the weather. One such example is the cricket. People thought that the cricket could help tell the outside temperature. As the story goes, the faster a cricket chirped, the warmer the temperature would be. The slower a cricket chirped, the cooler the temperature would be. You might try this for yourself: Use a watch with a second hand and count a cricket's chirps for 15 seconds. Is it warm or cool outside? Continue counting chirps for three days in a row. Did the chirps get faster when the weather was warmer?

Checking Comprehension

Write the answer to each question on the lines.

1. Why did people once use tales to predict weather?

   _____

   _____

2. Why do you think people still tell weather tales today?

   _____

   _____

Practicing Comprehension Skills

Choose a synonym for the underlined word. Fill in the correct circle.

3. Today, you can <u>switch</u> on the TV to hear the weather.

   ○ buy   ○ turn   ○ forget   ○ clean

4. There are many ways to <u>forecast</u> the weather.

   ○ have   ○ like   ○ remember   ○ predict

5. Weather <u>tales</u> are passed down from generation to generation.

   ○ stories   ○ songs   ○ tools   ○ houses

6. The warmer the temperature is, the <u>faster</u> a cricket chirps.

   ○ slower   ○ louder   ○ quicker   ○ quieter

7. Can a cricket help <u>tell</u> the outside temperature?

   ○ report   ○ change   ○ make   ○ use

8. Many weather sayings sound <u>unbelievable</u>.

   ○ common   ○ likely   ○ unlikely   ○ funny

Each word below was used in this article. On the line next to the word, write a synonym from the list that might have been used in its place.

9. insects   _____

10. chirped   _____

11. true   _____

12. many   _____

13. warmer   _____

> real
> bugs
> several
> hotter
> peeped

Practicing Vocabulary

Choose the word from the box that best matches each definition.
Write the word in the chart.

> discovered   retold   generation   attention   settlers   weather   unbelievable

Word	Meaning
14. _____	told again
15. _____	early families who came to America
16. _____	what it's like outside
17. _____	found
18. _____	careful thinking or listening
19. _____	not real
20. _____	age group

Writing a Journal Entry
Write a journal entry to describe today's weather. Use words like *windy, rainy, sunny*. Use a thesaurus to find synonyms so you have many choices of words to use.

Antonyms

How would you describe yourself? Are you funny or serious? Are you cheerful or grumpy? Are you outgoing or shy? The words *funny* and *serious*, *cheerful* and *grumpy*, and *outgoing* and *shy* have opposite meanings. These words are called **antonyms**.

Antonyms are words that are opposites. Knowing about antonyms can help you understand what you read and can help you use clear describing words when you write.

Read the two paragraphs below. Notice how antonyms create two very different scenes.

The temperature had dropped to record-breaking lows, and Len felt as if his whole body would freeze. He wore his heaviest clothes and tried to stay active while waiting for the bus. Oh, I wish it were summer again! Len sighed.

The temperature had soared to record-breaking highs, and Len felt as if his whole body would melt. He wore his lightest clothes and tried to stay still while waiting for the bus. Oh, I wish it were winter again! Len sighed.

Reread the paragraphs to find the antonym for each word listed below. Write the antonym on the line.

soared   _____

highs   _____

melt   _____

lightest _____

still   _____

summer   _____

Tip

Recognizing antonyms and their meanings will help you understand what you read and choose the best words when you write.

DESERTS HOT & COLD

Does the word desert make you picture vast sands under a blazing sun? You may be picturing the Sahara Desert of northern Africa. That is the largest desert in the world. The Sahara does, indeed, have sandy areas, but the sun is not always blazing. Saharan daytime temperatures may rise above 100 degrees Fahrenheit, but after sunset, the air cools rapidly. Temperatures can then fall well below freezing.

The Sahara is an example of a hot desert. In hot deserts, air temperature drops quickly at night and climbs quickly after sunrise. Another hot desert is the Mojave Desert of North America. One deep area of the Mojave has such uncomfortable heat in summer, it is known as Death Valley. Even in Death Valley's hottest months, nighttime temperatures dive to a comfortable level.

Most deserts are hot, but there are cold deserts, too. High above sea level stretches the Gobi Desert of Central Asia. The Gobi usually has bitter cold and fierce winds. Yet daytime temperatures in summer reach over 100 degrees Fahrenheit! The Gobi is a harsh land. It can seem gentle when compared with the harshest, coldest desert in the world, the continent of Antarctica.

It might seem odd to call ice-covered Antarctica a desert, but *desert* is a suitable label. To be called a desert, a land area must receive fewer than ten inches of rain or snow a year. Antarctica receives fewer than three inches. Antarctica, the coldest land on Earth, is also one of the world's driest deserts.

Checking Comprehension

Write the answer to each question on the lines.

1. Why is "Deserts, Hot and Cold" a good title for the article?

   _____

   _____

   _____

2. What is the difference between a desert and other lands?

   _____

   _____

   _____

Practicing Comprehension Skills

Read each sentence. Underline the two words that are antonyms.
Don't forget that antonyms are opposites.

3. Daytime in the desert is greatly different from nighttime.

4. Temperatures rise rapidly and then fall.

5. Uncomfortable daytime heat changes to a comfortable level at night.

6. The air cools after sunset, but temperatures climb after sunrise.

7. A blazing sun and freezing air are both found in deserts.

8. The harsh Gobi Desert seems gentle when compared with the Antarctic.

9. Deserts can be the hottest and the coldest places on Earth.

Complete the sentence by choosing the antonym for the underlined word. Fill in the circle by the answer.

10. A desert may seem <u>harsh</u>, but it can also be _____ .
    ○ fierce   ○ bitter   ○ punishing   ○ gentle

11. Is it <u>odd</u> to call Antarctica a desert, or is it a _____ name?
    ○ suitable   ○ label   ○ usually   ○ even

12. In a desert, air temperatures <u>drop</u> quickly and _____ quickly at different times of the day.
    ○ rapidly   ○ climb   ○ cools   ○ reach

Practicing Vocabulary

Write the word from the box that matches each clue.

usually	driest	areas	harsh	rapidly	compared	vast

13. antonym for mild   _____

14. antonym for rarely   _____

15. antonym for tiny   _____

16. antonym for slowly   _____

17. antonym for wettest   _____

18. synonym for places   _____

19. synonym for matched   _____

Writing a Paragraph to Compare and Contrast
Think about two people you know, two places you have visited, or two things you enjoy doing. On another piece of paper, write a paragraph about one of these subjects. Use antonyms to point out the differences.

Using Simile and Metaphor

Authors make their writing interesting by using comparisons to describe characters and things. One way an author can describe something is by saying that one is like the other. This kind of comparison uses the word *like* or *as* and is called a **simile**. This sentence is a simile: *The fog was as thick as pea soup.*

Another way an author can describe something is by saying one thing is another. This kind of comparison does not use *like* or *as* and is called a **metaphor**. This sentence is a metaphor: *The forest fire is a giant dragon.*

Read about a tall tale character named Mike Fink.
Look for similes and metaphors that help describe him.

The first time I met my new boss, Mike Fink, I thought he was as mean as a rattlesnake. When Mike Fink spoke, his voice rumbled like thunder. The ground would shake and so would we!

Once I got to know Mike Fink, I discovered he wasn't so bad. He was just a bundle of energy who needed to keep busy. One minute he would be helping us haul logs down the river, and the next minute he would be working in the kitchen flipping pancakes like flying saucers. After weeks of work I decided that working for Mike Fink was a very interesting job. Not everyone has a twisting tornado for a boss!

Fill in the circle next to the meaning of the metaphor and simile.

Mike Fink was a twisting tornado.

○ Mike Fink liked to twist. ○ Mike Fink was very busy.

○ Mike Fink saw a tornado. ○ Mike Fink liked storms.

When Mike Fink spoke, his voice rumbled like thunder.

○ Mike Fink had a sore throat.

○ Mike Fink was afraid of thunder.

○ Mike Fink spoke in a very loud voice.

○ Mike Fink heard rumbling.

Tip

When you read, look for comparisons that are similes and metaphors. Use them to help you picture in your mind what is being described.

STRATEGY: Using Figurative Language: Simile/Metaphor

PAUL BUNYAN LOOKS FOR A JOB

Paul Bunyan was one big baby! Some say he weighed 86 pounds at birth, give or take 10 pounds or so. His ma really had a hard time keeping him fed. He didn't eat like a horse. He ate like 20 horses!

Paul grew as fast as a bean vine in July, so he needed a new pair of boots every day! Now, this might be bending the truth a bit, but it has been said that he was so tall that most people had to yank the bottom of his pants just to get his attention!

Finally one day, Paul quit growing and went off to see the world. His dream was to be a logger. When he got to a logging camp, Paul decided to put on a show. "I can chop down more trees with one swing of my ax than you and your crew can chop down all day," Paul said to the boss.

Before the boss could finish laughing, Paul swung his ax like a lightning bolt. When he was through, twenty trees were down. Paul was a buzz saw of a logger.

After working at logging, Paul decided to move on to mining. He walked across the country in less than a week and reached the mines. The only problem was that Paul was a freight train standing on its end, so he couldn't fit into a mine. Then he moved on to the Mississippi River, hoping to be a steamboat captain. That didn't work because each time he stepped on the side of a boat, the boat flew into the air like a grasshopper!

"Hmm," Paul said to himself. "What shall I try now?"

Checking Comprehension

Write the answer to the question on the lines.

1. Why did Paul Bunyan keep moving from job to job?

_____

2. Was Paul Bunyan a real person? Explain your answer.

_____

_____

_____

Practicing Comprehension Skills

Fill in the circle next to the meaning of the simile and metaphor.

3. He ate like twenty horses.

    ○ He ate a lot of food.   ○ He ate with bad manners.

    ○ He ate near horses.   ○ He ate very little.

4. Paul was a freight train standing on its end.

    ○ Paul was standing.   ○ Paul sounded like a train.

    ○ Paul was very tall.   ○ Paul liked trains.

Read each description. Underline the two things being compared.
Circle **Simile** or **Metaphor**. Write the meaning of the sentence.

Comparison		Meaning
5. <u>Paul</u> grew as fast as a <u>bean vine</u> in July.	Simile Metaphor	_____ _____
6. <u>Paul</u> was a <u>buzz saw</u> of a logger.	Simile Metaphor	_____ _____

STRATEGY: Using Figurative Language: Simile/Metaphor

Write a simile and a metaphor to describe Paul Bunyan's size.

7. Paul Bunyan was as tall as a _____

8. Paul Bunyan was a _____

Write a simile and a metaphor to describe how Paul Bunyan worked.

9. Paul was as fast as _____

10. Paul was a _____

Write a simile and a metaphor to describe Paul Bunyan's appetite.

11. Paul was as hungry as _____

12. Paul was a _____

Practicing Vocabulary

Write a word from the box next to its definition.

yank	logger	lightning	freight	steamboat	through	week

_____ 13. goods to be carried

_____ 14. period of seven days

_____ 15. pull or tug in a sudden way

_____ 16. a person who cuts down trees, a lumberjack

_____ 17. flash of electricity during a storm

_____ 18. boat powered by steam

_____ 19. from one end to another

Writing a Description
On another piece of paper, write a description of a job you like to do. Use a metaphor and a simile to describe how you perform this job.

LESSON 26

Using Maps

Authors sometimes include **maps** to help you understand what you are reading. A map is a drawing of an area or region. The **map key** tells what the symbols on the map mean. The **compass rose** helps give directions.

Knowing how to read a map is important because maps show where you are and help you find the way to other places. Looking at a map can make the ideas you read clearer and add information you need to know.

Look at the map. Then read the article. Use the map to help you understand what you read.

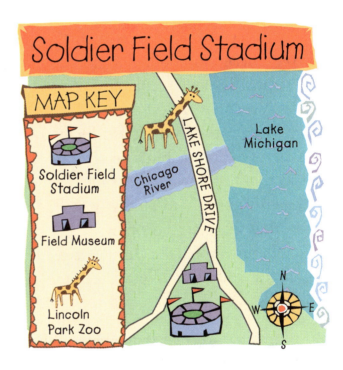

We're off to join 66,950 people to cheer for our favorite football team, the mighty Chicago Bears! We are traveling south on Lake Shore Drive and have already passed the Lincoln Park Zoo. There's the Chicago River to the west. Once we see the Field Museum, the next stop is Soldier Field Stadium!

Read the map to answer each question. Fill in the circle next to your answer.

What is located south of the Field Museum?

○ Soldier Field Stadium   ○ Chicago River

○ Lake Michigan   ○ Lincoln Park Zoo

When you leave Soldier Field, which direction would you go to get to the Lincoln Park Zoo?

○ east   ○ north

○ west   ○ south

Tip

If you are confused by something you read, looking at a picture, a chart, or a map can help you understand.

Read the article below. Use the map to help you locate places you are reading about.

ZOOMING in on LINCOLN PARK ZOO

Lincoln Park Zoo is our nation's oldest zoo. The idea for this fabulous zoo began over 100 years ago with an unusual gift to the city of Chicago in 1868. The gift was a pair of swans. Today, Lincoln Park Zoo is home to more than 1,000 animals, including birds at the Bird House. Here you can discover unique birds and do projects in the Bird Lab.

After a visit to the Bird House, you may want to walk west to drop by the Great Ape House. You'll see chimpanzees and the largest collection of gorillas in the United States.

One of the zoo's major goals is to rescue endangered animals and prepare them to return to the wild. Two endangered animals that live in the Antelope and Zebra House are the Grevy zebra and the Bactrian camel.

If you like big cats, you can backtrack to visit the Lion House. You may prefer to continue walking north to see what's happening at the Farm in a Zoo. Wherever you decide to spend time, you won't be disappointed when you visit this award-winning zoo! The zoo is open every day, and visitors are admitted free of charge.

Map Key

LINCOLN PARK ZOO

T Farm in a Zoo
Lion House
Antelope and Zebra House
Great Ape House
Gibbon Primate House
Bird House

To other animal habitats

Checking Comprehension

Write the answer to each question on the lines.

1. How might you convince someone to visit Lincoln Park Zoo?

_____

_____

2. What zoo attraction would you want to visit first? Why?

_____

_____

Practicing Study Skills

Read the map to answer the questions. Fill in the circle.

3. The Lion House is _____ of the Great Ape House.

   ○ east   ○ north   ○ south   ○ west

4. If you were at the Great Ape House and you wanted to see the zebras, which way would you go?

   ○ north   ○ south   ○ east   ○ west

5. The Gibbon Primate House is _____ of the Lion House.

   ○ north   ○ south   ○ east   ○ west

6. If you were at the Lion House and wanted to visit the lab in the Bird House, which way would you go?

   ○ east   ○ north   ○ south   ○ west

7. The Farm in a Zoo is _____ of the Antelope and Zebra House.

   ○ north   ○ south   ○ east   ○ west

8. To go from the Great Ape House to the Gibbon Primate House, you walk _____.

   ○ north   ○ south   ○ east   ○ west

9. How many animal habitats are shown on this map? _____

10. Are there other animal habitats in Lincoln Park Zoo? _____

11. How do you know?

   _____

   _____

12. Start at the Farm in a Zoo. Go south. What is your first stop?

   _____

13. If you go east of the Antelope and Zebra House, what is your next stop?

   _____

Practicing Vocabulary

Write a word from the box to go with each clue.

| rescue |
| collection |
| endangered |
| unique |
| admitted |
| prepare |
| award-winning |

14. group _____

15. save _____

16. given an honor or prize _____

17. at risk _____

18. allowed to enter _____

19. one of a kind _____

20. get ready _____

Writing a Descriptive Paragraph
Write a paragraph to describe the street where you live. Draw a picture map to go with it. Make a map key to tell what the pictures on your map stand for. Include a compass rose. Share your paragraph and map with a classmate.

Understanding Tables

Writers usually use words to give information to readers. Some ideas can be shown more clearly and quickly when they are in picture form. One type of picture that gives information is called a **table**. A table sorts and lists information in columns and rows. Each table has a title and headings. You can read down a column and across a row to learn different kinds of information.

Read the paragraph about space travel. What special information does the table give?

Twelve astronauts set foot on the moon between 1969 and 1972. No one has landed there since. Would you go if you had the chance? The moon is an airless and lifeless desert. Its gravity is very weak, and the temperature is either boiling or freezing. If you decide to go, put aside your sneakers, jeans, and T-shirts! You will need special clothing and your own supply of air!

Earth and Space Gear	
EARTH	**MOON**
jeans	water-cooled pants
T-shirt	suit with a computer
baseball cap	cap with a microphone and earphone
safety helmet for sports	bubble helmet filled with air
sneakers	boots attached to a suit

Write the answer to each question on the lines.

What is the purpose of the table?

_____

_____

What did you find out about clothing for moon travel?

_____

Tip

When you read a table, look at the title and headings. They will help you understand what the table is all about.

Read the article and look over the table. Think about how the table helps you understand what you read.

GRAVITY TUG OF WAR

There is a whole lot of spinning and orbiting going on in space. The moon orbits Earth, and Earth orbits the sun. This is also true for all the other planets and their moons. With all this spinning and orbiting going on, why doesn't everything crash into one another? The answer is gravity!

All objects pull other objects toward them. The more mass, or stuff, something is made of, the stronger the pull that object has. The Sun is the most gigantic object in our solar system. Its strong pull keeps all the planets in line.

It is the pull of Earth's gravity that keeps us from falling off our planet. When you weigh yourself, you are measuring the force with which gravity pulls on you to keep you on Earth. All planets have gravity, but the smaller a planet is, the weaker the gravity. The larger the planet is, the stronger the gravity. On which planet would you weigh more, Jupiter or Mercury?

Find Earth on the table and read across the row to find the number closest to your weight. Look up and down that column to determine what your weight would be on other planets.

YOUR WEIGHT ON NINE PLANETS					
Mercury	15	17	18	19	21
Venus	49	54	58	63	68
EARTH	55	60	65	70	75
Mars	20	22	24	26	28
Jupiter	128	140	152	163	175
Saturn	50	55	60	64	69
Uranus	43	47	51	55	59
Neptune	61	67	73	78	84
Pluto	2	2	2	2	3
WEIGHT IN POUNDS					

(PLANETS)

Checking Comprehension

Write the answer to each question on the lines.

1. The word *solar* means "having to do with the sun." Why do you think our planets with their moons are called the solar system?

   _____

   _____

2. How would your life change if Earth became the size of Pluto?

   _____

   _____

Practicing Study Skills

Use the table to answer the questions. Fill in the circle next to your answer.

3. On which planets would you weigh more?
   - ○ Neptune and Venus
   - ○ Jupiter and Neptune
   - ○ Mars and Saturn
   - ○ Jupiter and Venus

4. On how many planets would you weigh less?
   - ○ five
   - ○ seven
   - ○ six
   - ○ four

5. On which planets would you weigh nearly the same as what you weigh on Earth?
   - ○ Saturn and Venus
   - ○ Pluto and Jupiter
   - ○ Mars and Mercury

6. Which planet has the weakest gravity?
   - ○ Pluto
   - ○ Mercury
   - ○ Mars
   - ○ Venus

7. Which planet has the strongest gravity?
   - ○ Uranus
   - ○ Venus
   - ○ Neptune
   - ○ Jupiter

8. Which planet must be the smallest in size?
   - ○ Mercury
   - ○ Pluto
   - ○ Mars
   - ○ Saturn

What other information does the table tell you? Circle **YES** or **NO**.

9. You can tell which planets are smaller than Earth because you would weigh less on them.   **YES**   **NO**

10. As your weight changes on Earth, it would stay the same on the other planets.   **YES**   **NO**

11. Because of the pull of gravity, Earth must be the third largest planet.   **YES**   **NO**

Practicing Vocabulary

Choose the word from the box that matches each meaning.
Write the words to finish the table.

larger	closest	measuring	mass	orbiting	force	determine

	Word	Meaning
12.	_____	nearest
13.	_____	to find out by checking
14.	_____	power
15.	_____	finding the size or weight
16.	_____	bigger in size
17.	_____	size or bulk
18.	_____	moving in a circular path

Making a Poster
Choose a subject about outer space to write about and publish as a poster. You might write about planets, stars, astronauts, or Earth's moon. Include a table on your poster that gives some facts you found out about your subject.

Using Graphs

A **graph** is a quick way to find information. A graph uses bars or pictures to compare things, such as the sizes of dinosaurs or the number of points scored in a game.

When you see a graph, first look at its title. The title tells you what the graph is about. The words below the graph tell you what things are being compared. At the left are numbers that tell how fast, how big, or how many, depending on what the graph is about.

Read the article and study the graph to learn about how fast some animals move.

Do you think you can run fast? Lots of children your age can. You can probably run from one end of a football field to the other and back in about one minute. Most people would say that sounds pretty fast. Have you ever wondered whether a person could outrun a grizzly bear, a lion, or a greyhound dog? Look at the graph to learn the speeds at which some animals move.

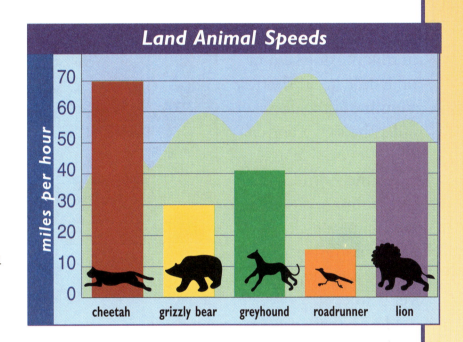

Land Animal Speeds

Write true or false on the lines. Use the graph to help you.

_____ A grizzly bear is faster than a greyhound.

_____ A lion can outrun a cheetah.

_____ A grizzly bear is twice as fast as a roadrunner.

_____ All the animals on the chart are faster than a person.

Tip

To find a number on a graph like this one, put your finger on a word at the bottom. Then follow the bar to the top and read the number on the left side.

Faster and Faster

Most people are interested in how fast things can go. Medals are given to athletes who ski down a mountain the fastest, skate around an ice rink the quickest, or run a mile in the shortest amount of time. People under their own power will never be able to match the swiftness of some animals, but with the help of vehicles used for travel, people are now moving more rapidly than ever before.

How fast are people traveling? It is possible for people to move as fast as 1,400 miles per hour. They can move that fast if they happen to be passengers on a supersonic jet. Land travel has gotten faster, too. Japan's bullet trains are now traveling as fast as 150 miles an hour. This is about three times as fast as riding in a car. An even faster train of the future will be the maglev. In test runs it moved as fast as 300 miles an hour.

There are cars that are traveling faster and faster, too. The family car goes about 55 to 65 miles an hour on highways. Professional race-car drivers are carefully trained to drive cars that go much faster. Their race cars can travel 150 to 200 miles an hour.

Do people really need to move so quickly? There are times when people need to find the fastest way to travel from one place to another, such as for a job or a vacation. Then the quickness of high-speed vehicles is helpful. There are other times when people simply find excitement in breaking speed records. For many reasons, people will continue to move faster and faster in the world.

Land Vehicle Speeds

vehicle:
- racing car — 200 miles per hour
- family car — 75 miles per hour
- bullet train — 150 miles per hour
- maglev — 300 miles per hour

miles per hour: 0, 50, 100, 150, 200, 250, 300

Checking Comprehension

Write the answer to each question on the line.

1. Tell in your own words what the article "Faster and Faster" was about.

   _____

   _____

2. Do you expect trains, planes, and automobiles to be even faster in the future? Why or why not?

   _____

   _____

Practicing Study Skills

Fill in the circle next to the right answer.

3. What does the bar graph show?
   - ○ speed records
   - ○ speeds of land vehicles
   - ○ trains
   - ○ cars

4. Which has the slowest speed?
   - ○ racing car
   - ○ maglev
   - ○ bullet train
   - ○ family car

5. Which has the greatest speed?
   - ○ racing car
   - ○ maglev
   - ○ bullet train
   - ○ family car

6. Which is a vehicle that carries one passenger at high speed?
   - ○ racing car
   - ○ maglev
   - ○ bullet train
   - ○ family car

7. Order the vehicles from slowest to fastest.
   Write 1, 2, 3, and 4 on the lines.

   ____ racing car   ____ family car

   ____ bullet train   ____ maglev

8. Why wouldn't you find ships and jet skis on this graph?

_____

9. Suppose you wanted to add supersonic jets to the graph. How would the bar for jets compare with the other bars in size?

_____

10. How would you change the title of the graph if supersonic jets were added?

_____

Practicing Vocabulary

Choose the word from the box that best matches each clue. Write the word on the line.

vehicles	quickness	excitement	miles
professional	supersonic	swiftness	

_____ 11. speed

_____ 12. distances are measured in these

_____ 13. fast motion

_____ 14. ships, planes, cars, trains

_____ 15. someone who does something as a job

_____ 16. faster than the speed of sound

_____ 17. something that stirs up or excites

Making a Graph
Find information about the speeds of some other things. On another piece of paper, write a paragraph that tells about the speeds you researched. Then make a graph to show your information.

Using a Dictionary

Sometimes when you are reading, you come to a word you don't know. Use a dictionary to help you. A dictionary is a book of words and their meanings. The words in a dictionary are listed in alphabetical order and are called **entry words**. At the top of each dictionary page, you will see **guide words** in large, dark type. These are the first and last entry words on that page.

Do you know what an armadillo is? Read the following passage and look at the photograph.

The early Spanish explorers discovered many interesting things in the New World. When these explorers first saw the animal we know as an armadillo, they were amazed. They thought the animal was wearing armor! They had never seen such an unusual animal!

There are no clues to tell you the meaning of the word *armor*. Read the following dictionary entry. Then decide which meaning of *armor* makes sense in the sentence.

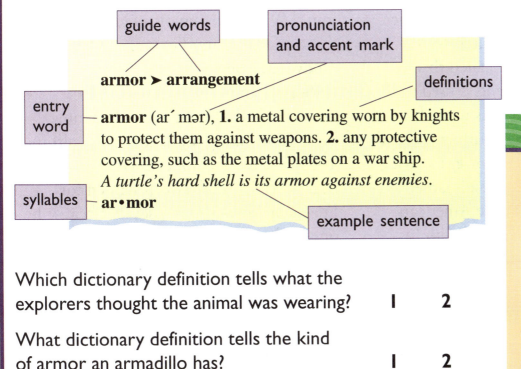

guide words	pronunciation and accent mark

armor ➤ arrangement

definitions

entry word — **armor** (ar´ mər), **1.** a metal covering worn by knights to protect them against weapons. **2.** any protective covering, such as the metal plates on a war ship. *A turtle's hard shell is its armor against enemies.*

syllables — **ar•mor**

example sentence

Tip

A dictionary can also help you learn how to say a word. Read how the word is divided into syllables. Stress the syllable with the accent mark when you say the word.

Which dictionary definition tells what the explorers thought the animal was wearing? **1   2**

What dictionary definition tells the kind of armor an armadillo has? **1   2**

On Your Own   Read about how some words have become part of the English language.

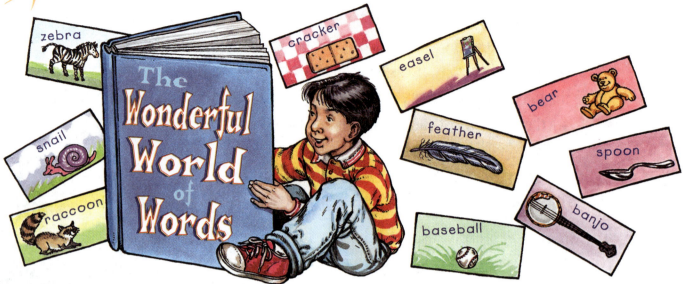

Do you speak a language other than English? If you use the words *piano, crayon,* and *parade,* you do! These words come from Italian, French, and Spanish.

Other English words have been borrowed from different languages. The word *easel* comes from a Dutch word meaning "donkey." It was called this because an easel has legs and is used to hold things. The *tulip* got its name from a Turkish word that means "turban," a kind of hat. That's because the flower looks a little like a turban. The animal name *raccoon* comes from a Native American word that means "he scratches with his hands." That's because raccoons use their paws to scratch tree bark and dig for food.

Not all English words come from other languages. Some words have been made by putting together two short words. A *classmate* is "a mate or friend in your class at school." Your *birthplace* is "the place of your birth, or where you where born."

Other words come from the names of places. *Tarantulas* get their name from Taranto, a town in Italy where they are found. When you enjoy a *hamburger,* think of Hamburg, Germany, where these sandwiches were first made.

Some people's names have even become words! Dr. Sylvester Graham believed in eating foods that are healthful. Today, we eat *graham crackers.* The toy bear we call a *teddy bear* is named for President Theodore Roosevelt, because he once refused to kill a bear cub while on a hunting trip.

Some dictionaries show where words came from. Try to find out where the words *guitar* and *banjo* came from. You may be surprised.

Checking Comprehension

1. How have so many words come into the English language?

   _____

   _____

2. Do you think new words are still becoming a part of the English language today? Why or why not?

   _____

   _____

Practicing Study Skills

Read the following dictionary entries. Then answer the questions.

bark ➤ barnacle **bark** (bärk) *noun* **1.** The outer covering of a tree. **2.** A type of sailing ship. *verb* **3.** to make the sound of a dog. **4.** To speak sharply. *The coach turned to bark angrily at the player.* **bark**	**tarantula ➤ tarry** **tarantula** (tə ran´chə lə) *noun* a large, hairy, poisonous spider whose bite is painful but not dangerous. **ta•ran•tu •la**

3. What are the two entry words shown on the dictionary pages?

   _____

4. What guide words would help you find each entry word?

   bark _____ **tarantula** _____

5. How many definitions are shown for each entry word?

   bark _____ **tarantula** _____

6. A bark can be a kind of _____ .
   ○ dog   ○ ship   ○ hat   ○ tree

Read the definition for each entry word. Then write your own sentence using each word.

7. tarantula

_____

8. bark (any definition)

_____

9. Which definition of bark did you use?

_____

Practicing Vocabulary

Choose the word from the box that belongs with each group.

| borrowed | classmate | birthplace | easel | hamburger | language | raccoon |

_____ **10.** friend, pal

_____ **11.** words, speaking

_____ **12.** squirrel, chipmunk

_____ **13.** paint, brush

_____ **14.** birth, birthday

_____ **15.** sandwich, hot dog

_____ **16.** took, used

Writing Riddles
Use a dictionary to help you find a word that has more than one meaning. Then write a word riddle on another piece of paper. Use the dictionary definitions to help you write the clues. Trade riddles with a friend.

Using an Encyclopedia

One kind of **encyclopedia** is a book or set of books with information on many subjects. Each book is called a **volume** and has a number and one or more letters on the spine. Each volume contains articles called **entries** that are arranged in alphabetical order.

To find an entry, use the volume with the letter that begins your subject name. The **guide word** at the top of each page names the first and last entries on the two pages. The entry words that name the articles on these pages are listed in alphabetical order.

To use an encyclopedia on the Internet, type a word in the **Search** box that names the subject. Then click on **GO**. The entry will appear on your screen.

Read the following encyclopedia entry from a set of books. Notice the features of the encyclopedia entry.

guide words

carnivorous plant

entry word

Carnivorous plant refers to any plant that captures insects for food. Carnivorous means meat-eating. To attract the meat (or insects), these plants are often bright-colored or sweet-smelling. Some carnivorous plants have sticky leaves to trap insects. Others have leaves shaped like a tube that hold rainwater or a liquid from the plant. Insects fall into these and drown.

entry

How would you find this entry in an encyclopedia that is a set of books?

_____

_____

How do the entry words help you?

_____

Tip

Some people like to use encyclopedias that are on the Internet or on CD ROM. Others prefer printed books. All three kinds of encyclopedia let you move easily from one entry to another.

Read these encyclopedia entries to find out about two kinds of carnivorous plants.

pitcher plant

Pitcher plant is an insect-eating plant named for its leaves, which are shaped like small jugs or pitchers with lids. Insects are attracted to these leaves by a special nectar. Insects that enter the top of the leaves are trapped by hairs or bristles that point downward. The trapped insect falls to the bottom of the leaves where the plant can use it for food.

Pitcher plants grow in areas around the world where there is a lot of moisture. Those that grow in North America are called New World pitcher plants. These plants grow to a height of 2 to 3 feet. The flowers can be purple or yellow.

Venus's-flytrap

Venus's-flytrap is an insect-eating plant that is found in the United States in North and South Carolina. It grows in wet, marshy areas where the soil has very little nitrogen. The plant traps and eats live insects to get what it needs to grow.

The plant grows to be about one foot high and

has small white flowers that are surrounded by unusual leaves. The leaves look like bear traps, with a hinge in the middle. Each half has hairs or bristles on its rim. When an insect touches the hairs, the leaves snap shut. Over time a liquid inside the leaf will change the soft parts of the insect into food. After seven to ten days, the plant will reopen its leaves to catch another meal.

Checking Comprehension

Write the answer to each question on the lines.

1. In what ways are the Venus's-flytrap and pitcher plant different from most other plants?

    _____

    _____

2. Do you think a Venus's-flytrap or a pitcher plant would make a good houseplant? Why or why not?

    _____

    _____

Practicing Study Skills

Answer the question about an encyclopedia that is a set of books.

3. Look at these volumes of an encyclopedia. How are they arranged?

    _____

4. Would you find *pitcher plant* and *Venus's-flytrap* in the same volume? Why or why not?

    _____

5. In which volume would each subject be found?

    pitcher plant _____   **Venus's-flytrap** _____

6. How can you find the entry once you have the correct volume?

    _____

7. What are the entry words for each encyclopedia article shown on page 122?

    _____   _____

Choose details from each encyclopedia article to fill in the diagram.
Tell how the two plants are alike and different.

pitcher plant   both   Venus's flytrap

8. _____   9. _____   10. _____

_____   _____   _____

_____   _____   _____

_____   _____   _____

different   same   different

Practicing Vocabulary

Write a word from the box to finish each sentence.

| bristles | marshy | moisture | nitrogen | reopen | nectar | unusual |

11. Most plants need a lot of _____ to grow.

12. Plants also need an element called _____ that is found in soil.

13. Some plants, like the Venus's-flytrap, have _____ leaves.

14. Morning glory flowers close at night and _____ in the morning.

15. A cactus has sharp little spikes that look like _____ .

16. Insects are attracted to the sweet liquid in flowers, called _____ .

17. Certain types of plants need to live in wet, _____ areas.

Writing an Article
On another piece of paper, write an article about another plant you think is interesting. Use the volumes of an encyclopedia or an encyclopedia on the Internet to find information.

Level C Glossary

A **accept** (ak sept') to take what is offered or given

admitted (ad mit' əd) allowed to go in

airborne (er' bôrn) floating or flying through the air

amazed (ə māzd') very surprised

animal (an' ə məl) any living being that can move by itself, has sense organs, and does not make its own food as a plant does

annoyed (ə noid') irritated, bothered, or angry

apartment (ə pärt' mənt) one large room or a group of rooms to live in

areas (er' ē əz) sections or regions of land

astronaut (as' trə nôt or as' trə nät) a person trained to make rocket flights in outer space

athletes (ath' lēts) people who are skilled at sports

attention (ə ten' shən) the act of noticing or observing

audience (ô' de əns or ä' de əns) a group of people who gather to hear and see a speaker, play, concert, or any similar kind of program

award-winning (ə wôrd' win' iŋ) having an honor or prize

awesome (ô' səm or ä' səm) causing a person to feel respect and surprise

B **balance** (bal' əns) the ability to keep the body steady without falling down

bared (berd) uncovered

baskets (bas' kəts) containers made by weaving together wood strips, straw, or grass

beast (bēst) any large four-footed animal

believe (bə lēv') to have trust in

birthplace (burth' plās) the place where a person was born

biscuit (bis' kit) a small, dry, crisp cake

borrowed (bär' od or bôr' od) taken and used as one's own

bristles (bris' əlz) short, stiff, prickly hairs

C **career** (kə rir') job or profession

celebrate (sel' ə brāt) to honor a special day with a party

centuries (sen' chər ēz) time periods of 100 years

ceremonies (ser'ə mō' nēz) acts done to celebrate a special occasion

championship (cham' pē ən ship') a contest to judge the best team in a sport

character (ker' ək tər) a person or animal in a story

chef (shef) a cook

chewed (chood) bit and ground up with the teeth

classmate (klas' māt) a member of same class at a school

closest (klōs' əst) nearest to

code (kōd) a system of secret writing in which letters are given special meanings

collection (kə lek' shən) a group of things gathered in one place

company (kum' pə nē) friends or companions

compared (kəm perd') looked at two or more things to see how they are alike or different

complaining (kəm plān' iŋ) finding fault with something

compute (kəm pyoot') to figure something out

confident (kän' fi dənt) sure; certain

constantly (kän' stənt lē) all the time

continued (kən tin' yood) kept on doing

creations (krē ā' shənz) things that are made

crust (krust) the crisp bottom part of a pizza

D **danger** (dān' jər) a condition in which something bad or harmful could happen

dangerous (dān' jər əs) likely to cause harm or pain

delicious (dē lish' əs) tasting very good

description (də skrip' shən) telling or writing about a person or thing using many details

designs (dē zinz') plans that must be followed in order to make something

determine (de tur' min) to find out exactly

disasters (di zas' tərz) happenings that cause much damage or suffering

disbelief (dis bə lēf') not accepting something as true

discovered (di skuv' ərd) found out; learned

dives (dīvz) goes headfirst

driest (drī' əst) having the least rain or water

125

E **easel** (ē′ zəl) a standing frame for holding a painter's canvas or a picture

encouragingly (en kur′ ij iŋ le) in a way that makes someone feel more confident

endangered (en dān′ jərd) in danger of becoming extinct or dying off

excitement (ek sīt′ mənt) the condition of feeling strongly about something

experimenting (ek sper′i ment iŋ) doing tests to find out or prove something

explosion (ek splō′zhən) the act of blowing up with a loud noise

F **famous** (fā′ məs) talked about or known by many people

faraway (fär′ ə wā) seeming to be distant

farthest (fär′ thəst) the greatest distance

favorable (fā′ vər ə bəl) good or pleasing

favorite (fā′ vər it) a person or thing liked best of all

female (fē′ māl) belonging to the sex that gives birth or produces eggs

fever (fē′ vər) great excitement

flipped (flipt) tossed or moved something with a quick jerk

floating (flōt′ iŋ) moving slowly through the air

followed (fä′ lōd) went after

force (fors) the power to cause motion or to stop or change motion

forward (fôr′ wərd) a player in or near the front of the team

fossil (fäs′ əl) the remains, prints, or traces of plants or animals that lived long ago

freezer (frē′ zər) a refrigerator that is used to store frozen things

freight (frāt) carrying goods

frightening (frīt′ n iŋ) making afraid

frowned (fround) to show that one dislikes or does not approve

funnel (fun′ əl) something having the shape of a cone with the widest part at the top

G **generation** (jen′ ər ā′ shən) a single stage in the history of a family

genuine (jen′ yo͞o in) really being what it seems to be; not false

giant (ji′ ənt) very large

glittered (glit′ ərd) shined with a sparkling light

grain (grān) the small, hard seed of wheat, corn, rye, or other cereal plants

gratefully (grāt′ fə lē) in a way that shows thanks

gravity (grav′ i tē) the natural force that draws objects toward the center of Earth

gripped (gript) took hold of

groom (gro͞om) to make neat and tidy

gulped (gulpt) swallowed quickly

H **hamburger** (ham′ burg ər) a sandwich that is made of a patty of cooked ground beef, usually in a round bun

hard (härd) using energy and effort

harsh (härsh) rough and causing pain

haze (hāz) confusion

helmet (hel′ mət) a hard hat to protect the head

helpless (help′ ləs) not able to take care of one's own needs

he's (hēz) contraction for he is

howled (hould) made a long cry

I **iguana** (i gwä′ nə) a large lizard of Central and South America

imagined (i maj′ ind) made a picture or idea in the mind

improved (im pro͞ovd′) became better

improvement (im pro͞ov′ mənt) the act of becoming better

instructor (in struk′ tər) a person who instructs; a teacher

invented (in vent′ əd) made or thought of something that did not exist before

J **joey** (jō′ ē) a baby kangaroo

K **knuckles** (nuk′ əlz) joints of the fingers

L **language** (laŋ′ gwij) human speech or writing

larger (lär′ jər) bigger in size

latched (lacht) fastened; locked

leather (leth′ər) a material made from the skin of cows, horses, goats, or other animals

lightning (līt′ niŋ) a flash of light in the sky

listened (lis′ ənd) paid attention in order to hear

lives (līvz) periods of time that a person or animal is alive

logger (lôg′ ər) a person who cuts down trees and takes the logs to a sawmill

M

marshy (mär′ she) like a swamp or other wet, soft land

mass (mas) a great size or bulk

masterpiece (mas′ tər pēs) the best thing that a person has ever made or done

measuring (mezh′ ər iŋ) finding out the size, amount, or extent of something

mention (men′ shən) to speak about in only a few words

message (mes′ ij) words sent from one person to another

miles (mīlz) measures of distance equal to 5,280 feet or 1.6093 kilometers

modern (mäd′ ərn) of or having to do with the present time or the period we live in

moist (moist) damp or a little wet

moisture (mois′ chər) water or other liquid that is in the air or the ground, or that forms tiny drops on a surface

motion (mō′ shən) movement from one place to another

N

nations (nā′ shənz) countries; groups of people living together in a certain area under one government

nectar (nək′ tər) the sweet liquid in many flowers, made into honey by bees

newspaper (no͞oz′ pā′ pər or nyo͞oz′ pā′ pər) a number of large folded sheets of paper printed with news, opinions, advertising, and other information

nitrogen (nī′ trə jən) an odorless, tasteless gas that makes up almost four-fifths of the air around Earth and is found in all living things

normal (nôr′ məl) usual; regular

noticed (nōt′ ist) paid attention to; saw

O

orbiting (ôr′ bit iŋ) moving in a path around a planet or other body in space

ordinary (ôrd′ n er′ ē) usual, regular, or normal

P

pale (pāl) having skin color that is lighter than usual because of a strong feeling

paleontologist (pāl′ē ən täl′ ə jist) a scientist who studies fossils

pavement (pāv′ mənt) a surface covered with asphalt, concrete, or bricks; for example, a road or sidewalk

peaceful (pēs′ fəl) quiet and calm; not liking to fight

peered (pird) looked closely in order to see better

petals (pet′ lz) the colored parts of a flower

playful (plā′ fəl) liking play or fun

poems (pō′ əmz) pieces of writing in which the words have a rhythm and often rhyme

polite (pə līt′) showing good manners

position (pə zish′ ən) a situation

practice (prak′ tis) doing something over and over again to become better at it

prehistoric (prē′ his tôr′ ik) time long ago before history was written

prepare (prē per′) to make ready

pressure (presh′ ər) force; weight

professional (prō fesh′ ən əl) earning a living from a sport or activity

proud (proud) feeling honored or pleased

Q

quickness (kwik′ nəs) speediness

R

raccoon (ra ko͞on′) a furry animal that has a long tail with black rings and black face markings that look like a mask

rapidly (rap′ id lē) quickly

released (rē lēst′) let go

remarkable (rē märk′ ə bəl) worth noticing because it is very unusual

reopen (rē ō′pən) open again

reported (rē pôrt′ əd) announced; told about an event

rescue (res′ kyo͞o) to free or save from danger, harm, or anything bad

restlessly (rest′ ləs lē) moving around in a worried way

retired (rē tīrd') stopped doing a job, especially because of getting older

retold (rē tōld') told again

scorer (skôr' ər) a player who makes points in a game

searches (sʉrch' əz) looks around in order to find a thing

settlers (set' lərz) people who go to live in a new country, colony, or region

shuttle (shut' l) a spaceship that travels into space and returns to Earth

shy (shī) easily frightened or scared

silverback (sil' vər bak') an older male gorilla who leads a troop

skeleton (skel' ə tən) the bones of an animal's body

smoothly (smōōth'lē) in an even, gentle way

sniffed (snifd) smelled by breathing air in through the nose

soared (sôrd) flew high in the air

spinning (spin' iŋ) turning; twisting

spreading (spred' iŋ) stretching out

stared (sterd) looked at for a long time with the eyes wide open

steamboat (stēm' bōt) a boat that is powered by water vapor

strike (strīk) the act of finding something valuable; for example, gold or oil

struggled (strug' əld) tried very hard

suddenly (sud' n lē) quickly

suggestion (səg jes' chən) an idea mentioned to another person about what that person should think about or do

supersonic (sōō'pər sän' ik) moving at a speed greater than the speed of sound

surrounded (sər round' əd) having something all around; in the middle of

swiftness (swift' nəs) speed

tank (taŋk) a glass box for keeping an animal

teammates (tēm' māts) members of the same team

temperature (tem' prə chər or tem' pər ə chər) the degree of heat or cold in something

through (thrōō) from one end to the other

thunderstorm (thun' dər stôrm) a storm that has thunder and lightning

tiny (tī' nē) very small

tornado (tôr nā' dō) a column of air that is spinning very fast

tossing (tôs' iŋ) throwing from the hand in a light, easy way

touches (tuch' əz) small changes or details

trail (trāl) a path

train (trān) to teach, or give practice in, some skill

troop (trōōp) a group of gorillas who live together

turquoise (tʉr' kwoiz or tʉr' koiz) greenish blue

unable (un ā' bəl) not having the means or power to do something

unbelievable (un' bə lēv' ə bəl) seeming not to be true

unique (yōō nek') unusual; remarkable; one of a kind

unusual (un yōō' zhōō əl) not usual or common, rare

usually (yōō' zhōō ə lē) in the normal or regular way

valentine (val' ən tīn) a card sent to a sweetheart on Valentine's Day; also, a sweetheart

varsity (vär' si tē) representing a school in games against others

vast (vast) very large

vehicles (vē' i kəlz or vē' hi kəlz) things used for carrying persons or things over land or space

veterinarian (vet' ər i ner' ē ən) a doctor who treats animals

visit (viz' it) to go to see someone

weather (weth' ər) the conditions outside (for example, temperature, sunshine, rainfall) at any particular time and place

week (wēk) a period of seven days

whiskers (hwis' kərz or wis' kərz) long, stiff hairs near the mouth of certain animals

wolves (wōōlvz) wild animals that look like dogs

wouldn't (wōōd' nt) contraction for would not

yank (yaŋk) to give a sudden, strong pull